RESEARCH METHODS

The Concise Knowledge Base Workbook

RESEARCH METHODS

The Concise Knowledge Base Workbook

James P. Donnelly
University at Buffalo,
State University of New York

William M. K. Trochim
Cornell University

Cincinnati, Ohio
www.atomicdog.com

ISBN 1-59260-163-4

Library of Congress Control Number: 2004115963

Printed in the United States of America by Atomic Dog Publishing, 1148 Main Street, Third Floor, Cincinnati, OH 45202-7236

10 9 8 7 6 5 4 3 2 1

Contents

Preface

"THE ROAD TO RESEARCH"

Introduction

The preface to the *Research Methods: The Concise Knowledge Base Workbook* introduces the metaphor of the "research road." This is the idea that the research process consists of a series of planned actions leading to a conclusion, much like travel is based on a series of predictable steps leading to a destination. The similarities between research and travel will allow you to think about the process of doing research as a series of steps leading to a successful study, just as a successful vacation results from good planning (and good luck and timing, which we can't help you with, but of course it is, you guessed it, also like research!). Concretely speaking, some of the major parallels between research and travel can be described in the kind of table presented here (you'll later find out just how much researchers love tables like this). We hope that by doing the exercises in the workbook, you will find that research need not be the "road less traveled."

When planning a trip, you ask:	Part in Text	When planning a study, you ask:
Where do you want to go?	Foundations	Where do things stand on a research problem, and where should they go?
Who do you want to take with you?	Sampling	Who will participate in the study?
How will you record your journey?	Measurement	How will you measure the results?
What will be on your itinerary?	Design	What procedures will you use?
How will you know whether it was a good trip?	Analysis	How will you know whether the study was successful?
What do you want to say about your trip?	Chapter 13, Write-Up	Where and how should you share your study?

THE PURPOSE OF THE *RESEARCH METHODS: THE CONCISE KNOWLEDGE BASE WORKBOOK*

The purpose of this workbook is to provide you with a learning "vehicle" to facilitate your trip down the research road. You might think of it as analogous to the kind of travel guide you might get to help you plan a trip. Our intention is to provide practical exercises to prepare you for your eventual excursion into the world of research. Just as each country has its own language and customs, so does the world of research. The workbook is structured to help you to "talk the talk" (the language) as well as "walk the walk" (the culture) of the professional researcher.

THE STRUCTURE OF THE *RESEARCH METHODS: THE CONCISE KNOWLEDGE BASE WORKBOOK*

The topics in the *Research Methods: The Concise Knowledge Base Workbook* parallel the *Research Methods: The Concise Knowledge Base* textbook. Each chapter is represented in this workbook with learning goals, exercises, and self-evaluations that correspond to the topics in the *Research Methods: The Concise Knowledge Base* textbook. The workbook is a collection of learning activities organized around five key aspects of doing research:

1. **Language.** In the beginning of your study of research methods, you might find yourself surprised by the number of unfamiliar terms you come across in class discussions and in your reading. The language exercises in the workbook will help to increase your fluency in this specialized form of communication.

2. **Concepts.** As a new researcher, you will be challenged not only to learn the language, but also to understand the bigger picture concepts that researchers use and discuss. These exercises are designed to give you additional exposure to concepts and to allow you to work with them in practical ways.

3. **Skills.** Ultimately, doing research requires proficiency in specific skills, just as any other human activity does, from cooking to flying an airplane. In fact, this workbook might have been titled *The Research Methods Skills Base*. And, as in other activities, "practice makes perfect" (or at least "pretty good"!).

4. **Products.** Every research study will have a beginning and an end. Most often, the end product is a written report. It is possible, however, to conceive of each step in the research process as having a product, so this workbook has been designed to help you have a concrete product for each chapter. These products might be seen as separate assignments, but they have an overall goal of helping you to build a research proposal, one of the most important kinds of documents in the world of research.

5. **Journal.** The workbook chapter products might be thought of as the objective outcome of the workbook. But there is a very important subjective side to doing research. The subjective aspect includes such things as your attitude about research, your feelings before and after you've learned something, and your sense of confidence and competence in research. The latter item reflects something called "research self-efficacy," which means the degree to which you believe you can successfully conduct the behavior needed to complete a task in research. The workbook will give you an opportunity to reflect on your research self-efficacy as you go through it. We call this section the "Journal" because you will also have a chance to jot down any insights, ideas, questions, plans, or other reactions to your reading and your research methods course. You will probably find that research is a very personal kind of experience, so we hope this part of the workbook will help you to make your learning meaningful and memorable.

part 1

FOUNDATIONS

1   **Foundations**

1

Foundations

Chapter Outline

1-1 THE LANGUAGE OF RESEARCH

A student once came to one of us with a worried look after a class lecture early in the semester. When asked what the trouble might be, she exclaimed, "I don't know any of these words! How can I understand the book or what you are talking about?!?!" This student was unhappily confronting the reality that researchers have a specialized language. She had come to graduate school to learn how to become a better counselor but soon found out that counseling has a scientific basis and that the language of science was quite foreign to her. Suddenly, a major obstacle appeared and her pursuit of her career goals seemed to be threatened. This was not the first, only, or last student to discover research anxiety, but we hope the exercises here will help to build the confidence needed to continue.

The best way to conquer research anxiety and begin transforming the research process into a more enjoyable activity is through the development of competence, beginning with the language. In recognition of this, *Research Methods: The Concise Knowledge Base* offers sets of Key Terms at the beginning of each chapter. You can use the workbook to help you master them along with the online exercises. You will find that many terms have common meanings across various areas of science and others have very specific use in particular fields. We've designed some exercises to help you with both kinds of terms.

Exercise 1-1a The Key Terms *Preview*

Instructions. This exercise should be done before you read the chapter. Read every term in the Key Terms list. Now go back through the list again and identify up to 10 terms that you are unsure of so that you can pay special attention to them as you read. If you find that the entire list of key terms is unfamiliar, you should plan to read the chapter more than once and complete this exercise more than once as well. Write your preview terms in the following spaces:

Term 1:_____

Term 2:_____

Term 3:_____

Term 4:_____

Term 5:_____

Term 6:_____

Term 7:_____

Term 8:_____

Term 9:_____

Term 10:_____

Exercise 1-1b The Key Terms *Review*

Instructions. This exercise should be done after you read the chapter. The idea here is to see how much you've picked up to help you with the key terms you identified in your preview exercise. In the following spaces, write definitions of the terms in your own words. Try your best to do them by memory, but if you need to look them up again, go ahead and do so.

Term 1:_____Definition:_____

_____

Term 2:_____Definition:_____

_____

Term 3:_____Definition:_____

_____

Term 4:_____Definition:_____

_____

Term 5:_____Definition:_____

_____

Term 6:_____Definition:_____

_____

Term 7:_____Definition:_____

_____

Term 8:_____Definition:_____

_____

Term 9:_____Definition:_____

_____

Term 10: _____Definition:_____

_____

1-2 CONCEPTS

Exercise 1-2a Understanding and Communicating Key Ideas

Instructions. This exercise can be used to help you understand passages in *Research Methods: The Concise Knowledge Base*. You will need a partner for this exercise. Ideally, your partner would be a classmate in your research methods course or an advanced student. If a classmate or other fellow student is not available, you may try the exercise with another willing person. Feel free to draw pictures or make up examples to help you explain the idea.

1. **Identify** a passage in Chapter 1, "Foundations," of *Research Methods: The Concise Knowledge Base* that you would like to understand better. For example, you might pick "Patterns of Relationships" in section 1-1e, but any section of the chapter will do. Keep in mind that if you are unsure of several parts of the chapter, you should do the earlier ones first because understanding the latter ones might depend on how well you understand the earlier ones.

2. **Read** the passage aloud to your partner. You may read it more than once if your partner requests you to do so.

3. **Discuss** the passage. Ask your partner to tell you what she or he heard in her or his own words. Give your partner feedback about what you think is the accuracy of her or his comment. If you discover discrepancies between your understanding and your partner's, read the passage aloud again.

4. **Write** the passage in the space provided. You and your partner should write a summary of the passage in your own words. After you have finished writing, read your passage to your partner and then allow your partner to take a turn.

5. **Conclusion.** You and your partner should now ask the question, "OK, now do we get it?" The evidence of improvement is your mutual understanding, your ability to discuss the passage orally, and your ability to write a brief summary. If you find that the passage is still unclear, well, that's what professors, email, and questions are for!

Exercise 1-2b Understanding Research Ethics

All research must be guided by scientific and ethical principles. Professional organizations such as the American Psychological Association have developed codes of ethics based on careful consideration of such principles. Members of such organizations are expected to know and adhere to the ethics of their profession. In addition, all research conducted in the United States should be done under the oversight of a local ethics board, usually known as the Institutional Review Board or IRB. In this section of the workbook, you will be asked to familiarize yourself with the requirements of your local research ethics office and to complete a tutorial of the kind usually required of all researchers.

Locate your college's or university's IRB (both the physical office and its website) and review the requirements for prospective researchers. Complete the following to prepare yourself to be compliant with the ethical guidelines at your school.

1. Familiarize yourself with the board meetings and see whether you can attend one to observe and learn about the process.

2. Download any forms you may need to complete to submit a study proposal (usually referred to as a "protocol").

3. Complete an online research ethics tutorial. Your IRB probably requires this tutorial and may have links you can follow. In most cases the online tutorials provide you with a self-test and certification that you can print and submit with your study proposal. The link to a page devoted to ethics established by the National Institutes of Health is http://www.nih.gov/sigs/bioethics/casestudies.html. This certificate offered through the NIH course is acceptable to most university IRBs, but your school may have additional or different requirements. In any case, completing the online tutorial will familiarize you with ethical principles and their history and current use.

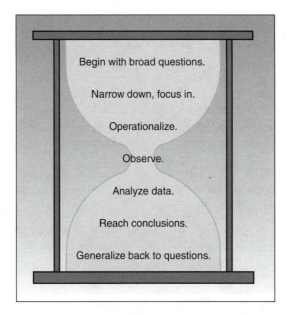

FIGURE 1-1
**The "Hourglass" Notion
of Research**

Exercise 1-2c Using the Hourglass

This exercise illustrates the universality of the structure of science. This structure is shown in Figure 1-1. Find a schedule of lectures on your campus or in your community and attend one with a scientific title, even if it is not in your field. As the speaker talks, fill in the blank outline of the hourglass model of research in the spaces provided with the terms used by the speaker for each step in the process.

Title of talk:

Presenter:

Date and location:

   1. Broad question:

   2. Focused question:

   3. Operations:

   4. Observations:

   5. Analysis:

   6. Focused conclusions:

   7. Broad conclusions:

Exercise 1-2d Practicing Critical Thinking about Study Type, Purpose, and Ethics

In this exercise, you will read brief descriptions of studies and then complete some items related to the design of the studies and ethical considerations.

1. A researcher was interested in the role of caffeine in sports performance. In cooperation with her university baseball team, she randomly assigned players to one of three conditions: (1) no caffeine (placebo condition), (2) low dose, (3) high dose. She then used performance on a batting machine as a test.

    a. What type of study (descriptive, relational, or causal) was this and why?

    b. What was the independent variable?

    c. What was the dependent variable?

    d. State a null and an alternative hypothesis for the study.

    e. Are there any ethical issues that should be considered in this study?

2. A professor was interested in student opinions about an upcoming election. He created a survey that asked about the favorability of various candidates and positions on issues. The survey also included some personal items so he could look at whether those characteristics were related to opinions.

    a. What type of study (descriptive, relational, or causal) was this and why?

    b. What was the independent variable?

    c. What was the dependent variable?

    d. State a null and an alternative hypothesis for the study.

    e. Are there any ethical issues that should be considered in this study?

3. A graduate student was interested in whether use of instant messaging by students was related to academic performance, attention span, and perceptions of social support. She interviewed classmates about their use of instant messaging, their grades, and their sense of support from friends. She also had them perform a brief task to estimate attention span.

    a. What type of study (descriptive, relational, or causal) was this and why?

    b. What was the independent variable?

    c. What was the dependent variable?

d. State a null and an alternative hypothesis for the study.

e. Are there any ethical issues that should be considered in this study?

4. A graduate student in music therapy wondered whether music therapy might be effective in reducing work stress. She identified a company that was willing to participate and then set up a voluntary session that was billed as a relaxation exercise. The participants completed a measure of work-related stress and mood before and after the music session.

a. What type of study (descriptive, relational, or causal) was this and why?

b. What was the independent variable?

c. What was the dependent variable?

d. State a null and an alternative hypothesis for the study.

e. Are there any ethical issues that should be considered in this study?

5. A researcher was interested in the quality of life of women with a certain disorder. She located an online support group and, with the permission of the group organizers, conducted an online discussion about the issues the women face and how these problems have affected their quality of life.

a. What type of study (descriptive, relational, or causal) was this and why?

b. What was the independent variable?

c. What was the dependent variable?

d. State a null and an alternative hypothesis for the study.

e. Are there any ethical issues that should be considered in this study?

Exercise 1-3a Choosing a Topic

The first task in a research project is to identify a topic. Sometimes students have too many topics in mind, so the task is to narrow the focus. If you are at square one and unsure where to begin, you might consider the following questions, noting any initial response you might have. Read about each suggested source and complete the suggested activities.

1. **Previous Studies.** If you have access to a library, we suggest you physically go there and begin browsing current journals with titles that seem to be interesting to you. If your professor has suggested specific journals, start there. If you are at a complete loss for where to start, try *The Psychological Bulletin*. Perusal of this journal will have some other benefits for the beginning researcher: You will see the state of the art in literature review methods, and you will be able to observe the interaction of theory, data, conclusion, and critique. That is, you'll see the authors doing their best to summarize the evidence on a particular topic and will also see how some other experts in the field see the issue.

   a. Exercise:

   i. What are the key journals in your topic area?

   1. _____

   2. _____

   3. _____

   4. _____

   5. _____

   ii. Try to locate the most recent reviews of your topic area using the following:

   1. *The Annual Review of Psychology*

   2. *The Psychological Bulletin*

   3. _____ (name of the specialty journal in your field that publishes reviews and meta-analyses)

2. **Personal and Societal Issues.** Quite often, personal experience leads one to the study of a particular field or issue. This experience may lead to a lifelong pursuit of knowledge and a productive line of research. It may also produce frustration if the issue is "too close for comfort." That is, if your daily life is dominated by a distressing personal issue, it is quite understandable that you might like to obtain the sort of knowledge that will increase your sense of control and decrease distress. However, the more direct route is to get help for the issue and *then* consider studying it. You might find that your focus shifts to less personal but socially important issues.

   a. Exercise: Make a list of personal and societal issues that you believe are of some significance and have potential for research:

   1. _____

   2. _____

   3. _____

   4. _____

d. State a null and an alternative hypothesis for the study.

e. Are there any ethical issues that should be considered in this study?

4. A graduate student in music therapy wondered whether music therapy might be effective in reducing work stress. She identified a company that was willing to participate and then set up a voluntary session that was billed as a relaxation exercise. The participants completed a measure of work-related stress and mood before and after the music session.

a. What type of study (descriptive, relational, or causal) was this and why?

b. What was the independent variable?

c. What was the dependent variable?

d. State a null and an alternative hypothesis for the study.

e. Are there any ethical issues that should be considered in this study?

5. A researcher was interested in the quality of life of women with a certain disorder. She located an online support group and, with the permission of the group organizers, conducted an online discussion about the issues the women face and how these problems have affected their quality of life.

a. What type of study (descriptive, relational, or causal) was this and why?

b. What was the independent variable?

c. What was the dependent variable?

d. State a null and an alternative hypothesis for the study.

e. Are there any ethical issues that should be considered in this study?

1-3 SKILLS

In addition to wading into the language of research methodology, you will soon be immersed in the literature of your topic area. For some of you, the major product of your first research course will be a literature review. Even if you are expected to write a proposal for research, you will have to begin with a "lit review." We hope the exercises here will get you off to a good start.

We live in an age of information overload, but developing good literature search habits will help you to minimize the number of dead ends and confusing forks in the road. And you undoubtedly have friends (perhaps many you haven't met yet) working to help you keep up with the information and information technology explosion in your local library. In addition, librarians and publishers are working together to try to make the best possible use of computer technology in managing the books, journals, and other information sources you will need to access on the research road. But the main constant of this technology is change, and it is inevitable that the databases you use today will soon be different in both content and function. However, good skills should be transferable as improvements in literature search technology evolve.

In the following exercises, you will get some practice in what we hope become good habits of literature searching. First, here is some general advice on searching the literature:

1. Start early! What does early mean? How about right after you finish reading this chapter? Searching the literature is easier than ever with the advent of searchable and full-text databases, but to do it well, you must allow time to obtain materials, to read and critique, and to conduct supplementary searches based on the reference lists of the studies you initially found.

2. Keep a record of the steps you take in searching the literature, including the databases you search, the keywords used, and any limits you might have set (e.g., dates, population limits). You should report your literature search procedures in your paper, and keeping a record of your steps will allow you to do so.

3. Get to know your local librarian.

4. Do not rely on full-text databases only.

5. Do not rely on only one reference database.

6. Do not rely on Google or other Internet search engines for your primary sources, but instead think of the Internet as a great complementary search tool for finding out about individuals and organizations with interests in your topic area. Personal and organizational web pages sometimes include citations or even downloadable articles.

7. Read before you copy or print. Ultimately, a carefully selected pile of articles will be easier to manage than a comprehensive pile containing a lot of papers for your recycling bin.

8. Consider using reference manager software. You can find several options in commercially available software, and theoretically, anyone could develop her or his own database using a spreadsheet program. Some of the more widely used programs are produced by a company called Thomson ISI ResearchSoft. You can obtain trial versions of programs it sells such as EndNote (http://www.endnote.com) and ProCite (http://www.procite.com). These programs allow you to directly download citations into a database (including the abstracts) and also offer writing help. One popular feature in EndNote is "Cite while you write." This feature allows you to choose a template according to the writing conventions of your field (e.g., APA, 5th ed.), formats your paper, and then allows you to insert citations while automatically building your reference list. You can download a fully functional 30-day trial of these programs free.

d. State a null and an alternative hypothesis for the study.

e. Are there any ethical issues that should be considered in this study?

4. A graduate student in music therapy wondered whether music therapy might be effective in reducing work stress. She identified a company that was willing to participate and then set up a voluntary session that was billed as a relaxation exercise. The participants completed a measure of work-related stress and mood before and after the music session.

a. What type of study (descriptive, relational, or causal) was this and why?

b. What was the independent variable?

c. What was the dependent variable?

d. State a null and an alternative hypothesis for the study.

e. Are there any ethical issues that should be considered in this study?

5. A researcher was interested in the quality of life of women with a certain disorder. She located an online support group and, with the permission of the group organizers, conducted an online discussion about the issues the women face and how these problems have affected their quality of life.

a. What type of study (descriptive, relational, or causal) was this and why?

b. What was the independent variable?

c. What was the dependent variable?

d. State a null and an alternative hypothesis for the study.

e. Are there any ethical issues that should be considered in this study?

1-3 SKILLS

In addition to wading into the language of research methodology, you will soon be immersed in the literature of your topic area. For some of you, the major product of your first research course will be a literature review. Even if you are expected to write a proposal for research, you will have to begin with a "lit review." We hope the exercises here will get you off to a good start.

We live in an age of information overload, but developing good literature search habits will help you to minimize the number of dead ends and confusing forks in the road. And you undoubtedly have friends (perhaps many you haven't met yet) working to help you keep up with the information and information technology explosion in your local library. In addition, librarians and publishers are working together to try to make the best possible use of computer technology in managing the books, journals, and other information sources you will need to access on the research road. But the main constant of this technology is change, and it is inevitable that the databases you use today will soon be different in both content and function. However, good skills should be transferable as improvements in literature search technology evolve.

In the following exercises, you will get some practice in what we hope become good habits of literature searching. First, here is some general advice on searching the literature:

1. Start early! What does early mean? How about right after you finish reading this chapter? Searching the literature is easier than ever with the advent of searchable and full-text databases, but to do it well, you must allow time to obtain materials, to read and critique, and to conduct supplementary searches based on the reference lists of the studies you initially found.

2. Keep a record of the steps you take in searching the literature, including the databases you search, the keywords used, and any limits you might have set (e.g., dates, population limits). You should report your literature search procedures in your paper, and keeping a record of your steps will allow you to do so.

3. Get to know your local librarian.

4. Do not rely on full-text databases only.

5. Do not rely on only one reference database.

6. Do not rely on Google or other Internet search engines for your primary sources, but instead think of the Internet as a great complementary search tool for finding out about individuals and organizations with interests in your topic area. Personal and organizational web pages sometimes include citations or even downloadable articles.

7. Read before you copy or print. Ultimately, a carefully selected pile of articles will be easier to manage than a comprehensive pile containing a lot of papers for your recycling bin.

8. Consider using reference manager software. You can find several options in commercially available software, and theoretically, anyone could develop her or his own database using a spreadsheet program. Some of the more widely used programs are produced by a company called Thomson ISI ResearchSoft. You can obtain trial versions of programs it sells such as EndNote (http://www.endnote.com) and ProCite (http://www.procite.com). These programs allow you to directly download citations into a database (including the abstracts) and also offer writing help. One popular feature in EndNote is "Cite while you write." This feature allows you to choose a template according to the writing conventions of your field (e.g., APA, 5th ed.), formats your paper, and then allows you to insert citations while automatically building your reference list. You can download a fully functional 30-day trial of these programs free.

9. See whether any recent handbooks or major review articles have been published in your topic area. Recent dissertations in your area can also be invaluable in identifying sources.

10. Try to identify the key authors in your area. If you have access to the citation databases (ISI Web of Science that are widely available include the Science Citation Index and Social Science Citation Index), you can find the key researchers and their most frequently cited papers quickly.

11. Government sources can be very helpful. For example, the National Library of Medicine (http://www.nlm.nih.gov/hinfo.html), accessible from any Internet connection, provides you with access to PubMed, a database of more than 4,600 biomedical journals.

Exercise 1-3a Choosing a Topic

The first task in a research project is to identify a topic. Sometimes students have too many topics in mind, so the task is to narrow the focus. If you are at square one and unsure where to begin, you might consider the following questions, noting any initial response you might have. Read about each suggested source and complete the suggested activities.

1. **Previous Studies.** If you have access to a library, we suggest you physically go there and begin browsing current journals with titles that seem to be interesting to you. If your professor has suggested specific journals, start there. If you are at a complete loss for where to start, try *The Psychological Bulletin*. Perusal of this journal will have some other benefits for the beginning researcher: You will see the state of the art in literature review methods, and you will be able to observe the interaction of theory, data, conclusion, and critique. That is, you'll see the authors doing their best to summarize the evidence on a particular topic and will also see how some other experts in the field see the issue.

    a. Exercise:

    i. What are the key journals in your topic area?

    1. _____

    2. _____

    3. _____

    4. _____

    5. _____

    ii. Try to locate the most recent reviews of your topic area using the following:

    1. *The Annual Review of Psychology*

    2. *The Psychological Bulletin*

    3. _____ (name of the specialty journal in your field that publishes reviews and meta-analyses)

2. **Personal and Societal Issues.** Quite often, personal experience leads one to the study of a particular field or issue. This experience may lead to a lifelong pursuit of knowledge and a productive line of research. It may also produce frustration if the issue is "too close for comfort." That is, if your daily life is dominated by a distressing personal issue, it is quite understandable that you might like to obtain the sort of knowledge that will increase your sense of control and decrease distress. However, the more direct route is to get help for the issue and *then* consider studying it. You might find that your focus shifts to less personal but socially important issues.

    a. Exercise: Make a list of personal and societal issues that you believe are of some significance and have potential for research:

    1. _____

    2. _____

    3. _____

    4. _____

3. **Advisors and Other Faculty.** In many programs, students are drawn to advisors because of common interests, and this naturally leads to consideration of research topics. Joining an advisor who has expertise in a particular area can be a big help in jump-starting your research career. Sometimes you can become part of an ongoing study, and although you may not have the satisfaction of taking a project from idea to result, you will probably complete your first project much faster. This route may, in fact, be the most sensible if you have little or no prior experience in research. The skills gained will transfer readily to the next project. On the other hand, you might be in a department where advisor interests are divergent from your own. In that case, you can still find the closest approximation based on familiarity with a research method or population and form an effective partnership. Most faculty members enjoy helping students find their way in developing research interests. It is always wise to approach faculty in a respectful way and to show gratitude for whatever time and guidance can be shared.

   a. **Exercise:** Identify the faculty members most closely aligned with your topic area and obtain an example of something they have written on the topic. Most professors will freely share copies of their work. After you've read the article(s), consider making an appointment to discuss your reaction and ideas for future studies. Consider the following issues:

   i. Do you feel comfortable with this person?

   _____

   ii. Does this faculty member appear to be suitable in terms of receptivity to you and your ideas?

   _____

   iii. What practical limits might need to be considered (sabbatical, retirement, existing commitments to other projects and students)?

   _____

   _____

   _____

   _____

4. **Experts in the Field.** In the age of email, you are able to contact the leading scholars in the world in your field. The prospect of doing so should not be dismissed nor treated lightly. In our experience, you have better than a 50 percent chance of getting a reply for feedback about a topic if you identify a leading researcher at another institution. Doing some preliminary work is very important; for example, you need to find and review this person's work on a topic and carefully write your email so that it is concise, specific, and respectful. You want to make it as easy as possible for the person to reply in a helpful way and to write in a way that would encourage a reply. Remember the Golden Rule: Treat others the way you would like to be treated.

5. **Theories.** "Nothing is so practical as a good theory" (Lewin, 1951, p. 169). How can a theory be practical? By definition, a theory is a set of testable ideas about how something happens and what influences the way it happens. If you are writing a literature review or proposing study, you need to know the leading theories in your area. As you become familiar with theory, you may find yourself considering ways that the idea might apply to your own interest, or you may find yourself challenging prior thinking by coming up with an alternative notion about the phenomena.

a. **Exercise:** What are the leading theories in your topic area, and who are the leading researchers associated with each position?

i. Theory 1:_____
_____
_____
_____
_____
_____
_____

ii. Theory 2:_____
_____
_____
_____
_____
_____

iii. Theory 3:_____
_____
_____
_____
_____
_____

Lewin, K. (1951). *Field Theory in Social Science*. New York: Harper & Row.

Exercise 1-3b Narrowing Your Topic
to a Manageable Scope

The most frequent difficulty that students have at this stage is that they are interested in too many things. If this is the case, we suggest you do the following:

1. Make a list of all the topics you might be interested in studying.

2. Rank the topics in terms of your passion (or what you might hope it could become) for each topic and eliminate all but the top three.

3. Go through your *top three* and rate them on short-term feasibility and long-term potential for your research career. For the Feasibility (i.e., Is the study practical given your resources and circumstances?) and Potential (i.e., Does the topic offer future possibilities in terms of follow-up studies, publication, funding, or your long-term interests?) ratings, use this scale:

1 = Low	5 = Medium	10 = High

	Rank	Feasibility	Potential
Topic:_____	____	____	____
Topic:_____	____	____	____
Topic:_____	____	____	____
Topic:_____	____	____	____
Topic:_____	____	____	____
Topic:_____	____	____	____
Topic:_____	____	____	____
Topic:_____	____	____	____
Topic:_____	____	____	____
Topic:_____	____	____	____

Exercise 1-3b Searching Electronic Databases

In this exercise, you will try your hand at identifying related keywords and understanding their relationship to one another. Please note that many libraries include excellent online tutorials and workbooks with instructions on proper use of keywords in conducting literature searches. We strongly encourage you to explore the possibilities on your home college or university library website. In addition, we suggest you try this exercise. To complete it, you will need access to an electronic database such as PsycINFO or ERIC. The keywords in PsycINFO all come from an official thesaurus, called the *Thesaurus of Psychological Index Terms*. It is published by the American Psychological Association and was reissued in 2001. This book provides the current meaning of terms in psychology as well as the indexing of terms to one another. PsycINFO uses this index in mapping terms to a keyword search. Your task is to generate a map of terms that are connected to the PsycINFO database. An example follows:

Step 1: Enter a keyword and check "Map term to subject heading."

Step 2: Examine the map of related terms.

Step 3: Choose the related terms that appear to be relevant to your topic.

Step 4: Examine your options for limiting your search. If you have produced an unmanageable number of citations (many thousands), see what happens when you limit the set of references by such factors as publication year, publication type, language, type of article, and population.

1-4 PRODUCTS

At this point, if you have done all the exercises, you will already have several products:

1. The certification of your ethics training
2. A topic or topic list
3. An initial literature search
4. A reference manager and database
5. Critiques of one or more key articles in the literature

1-5 JOURNAL

Exercise 1-5a Research Methods Foundations Self-Efficacy Evaluation

Use the following scale to rate your skills in each of the areas listed.

1 = Little or no ability to perform this task
2 = Some ability to perform this task
3 = Moderately good ability to perform this task
4 = Very good ability to perform this task
5 = Excellent ability to perform this task

1. ____ Understand and use key terms in the foundations of research methods.

2. ____ Perform a literature search of relevant databases using appropriate keywords.

3. ____ Identify the major kinds of relationships found in nature and science.

4. ____ Write an hypothesis and an alternative.

5. ____ Describe the hourglass model of research.

6. ____ Identify the components of a study.

7. ____ Identify key concepts in research ethics.

8. ____ Find and complete an online tutorial in research ethics.

Exercise 1-5b Research Methods Foundations Self-Evaluation

In the space provided, jot down your personal reactions to Chapter 1, "Foundations," of *Research Methods: The Concise Knowledge Base*. What did you like best? What did you still need to study? How might you now improve your skills in the foundations of research methods?

S A M P L I N G

2

Sampling

Chapter Outline

2-1 THE LANGUAGE OF SAMPLING

Exercise 2-1a The Key Terms *Preview*

Instructions. This exercise should be done before you read the chapter. Read every term in the Key Terms list. Now go back through the list again and identify up to 10 terms that you are unsure of so that you can pay special attention to them as you read. If you find that the entire list of key terms is unfamiliar, you should plan to read the chapter more than once and complete this exercise more than once as well. Write your preview terms in the following spaces:

Term 1:_____

Term 2:_____

Term 3:_____

Term 4:_____

Term 5:_____

Term 6:_____

Term 7:_____

Term 8:_____

Term 9:_____

Term 10:_____

Exercise 2-1b The Key Terms *Review*

Instructions. This exercise should be done after you read the chapter. The idea here is to see how much you've picked up to help you with the key terms you identified in your preview exercise. In the following spaces, write definitions of the terms in your own words. Try your best to do them by memory, but if you need to look them up again, go ahead and do so.

Term 1:_____Definition:_____

_____

Term 2:_____Definition:_____

_____

Term 3:_____Definition:_____

_____

Term 4:_____Definition:_____

_____

Term 5:_____Definition:_____

_____

Term 6:_____Definition:_____

_____

Term 7:_____Definition:_____

_____

Term 8:_____Definition:_____

_____

Term 9:_____Definition:_____

_____

Term 10:_____Definition:_____

_____

2-2 CONCEPTS

Exercise 2-2a Understanding and Communicating Key Ideas

Instructions. This exercise can be used to help you understand passages in *Research Methods: The Concise Knowledge Base*. You will need a partner for this exercise. Ideally, your partner would be a classmate in your research methods course or an advanced student. If a classmate or other fellow student is not available, you may try the exercise with another willing person. Feel free to draw pictures or make up examples to help you explain the idea.

1. **Identify** a passage in Chapter 2, "Sampling," of *Research Methods: The Concise Knowledge Base* that you would like to understand better. Keep in mind that if you are unsure of several parts of the chapter, do the earlier ones first because understanding the latter ones might depend on how well you understand the earlier ones.

2. **Read** the passage aloud to your partner. You may read it more than once if your partner requests you to do so.

3. **Discuss** the passage. Ask your partner to tell you what she or he heard in her or his own words. Give your partner feedback about what you think is the accuracy of her or his comment. If you discover discrepancies between your understanding and your partner's, read the passage aloud again.

4. **Write** the passage in the space provided. You and your partner should write a summary of the passage in your own words. After you have finished writing, read your passage to your partner and then allow your partner to take a turn.

5. **Conclusion.** You and your partner should now ask the question, "OK, now do we get it?" The evidence of improvement is your mutual understanding, your ability to discuss the passage orally, and your ability to write a brief summary. If you find that the passage is still unclear, well, that's what professors, email, and questions are for!

Exercise 2-2b Gaining Practice in Sampling Critique

In Chapter 1, "Foundations," you began to think about *what* to study. In this one, you begin to consider *who* knows, has experience with, or can otherwise be studied to find the *what* you want to know more about. In Chapter 2, "Sampling," you read how researchers address the very real problem that you usually have to choose *some* participants from the general population you want to study. In just about every field of research from political science to biology, scientists study *samples* but are really interested in being able to talk about populations. That is, they want to make *general* statements about the problem they've identified. This is true except for the rare instances in which you have a whole population at your fingertips, or you have the resources to conduct a complete census of a large population like the U.S. Census Bureau. In the next exercise, you'll get some practice thinking about how you can make conclusions from studying samples and also what limits there might be (the *threats to external validity*). We'll consider situations that are relatively common in life so you can focus on the critical thinking rather than the details of an unfamiliar area of science. Several cases will be described, and then you'll be asked to think critically about the external validity issues in each case.

Case 1

A marketing firm develops a campaign for a new weight loss program. The campaign features testimonials from a few people who have successfully completed the program. The firm will have these "success stories" give brief statements about how much weight they've lost and note that they had tried other methods unsuccessfully before. The marketing firm decides to use some males and females between the ages of 30 and 50.

Sampling Critique

1. How would you describe the sampling strategy using the concepts from Chapter 2?

2. What is the population that the company hopes the sample will generalize to?

3. What are the limits or threats to the external validity of the sampling strategy?

Case 2

A new law was passed making it illegal to smoke in restaurants and bars. The law was unpopular with bar owners who feared the loss of business. They decided to get some "data" to help them in their fight to overturn the law. The month before the law was to take effect, the bar owners association surveyed the patrons of their establishments who were smoking and asked them what they thought about the new law. They reported the following results in their report: "We surveyed over 500 adults in 25 taverns across the state. We found that 100 percent of the people are against this law and ask the legislature to consider the opinions of the taxpayers in this state rather than the special interests of the health insurance industry."

Sampling Critique

1. How would you describe the sampling strategy using the concepts from Chapter 2?

2. What is the population that the bar owners say the sample will generalize to?

3. What are the limits or threats to the external validity of the sampling strategy?

Case 3

A graduate student wanted to study the quality of life of women with a chronic illness. She found an Internet-based support group for these women and received permission to invite the group members to visit the research website that she set up and answer her survey about their quality of life.

Sampling Critique

1. How would you describe the sampling strategy using the concepts from Chapter 2?

2. What is the population that the student hopes the sample will generalize to?

3. What are the limits or threats to the external validity of the sampling strategy?

2-3 SKILLS

The two main skills in sampling are being able to pick an appropriate sampling strategy and to estimate the number of participants you will need. The next two exercises will give you some practice with each of these skills, though you will learn more about calculating sample size in a subsequent chapter.

Exercise 2-3a Examining the Consequences of Choosing a Sampling Procedure

Excerpts from several published studies are reprinted here. Read each one and then answer the questions that follow.

Study 1.   Alcohol use in college. (Yu, Evans, & Perfetti, 2003)

Prior studies have shown that many college students engage in heavy drinking and that such drinking may lead to alcohol-related problems. This study examined treatment-seeking attitudes among students in relation to their alcohol education background, alcohol environment, alcohol consumption, and perceived and actual drinking problems. A sample of 878 students from five New York State colleges were randomly selected through the use of complete student telephone directories provided by students' colleges for a telephone interview. The results indicated that alcohol education was associated with positive attitudes toward treatment and this may be important in efforts to reduce drinking related problems on campuses.

Sampling Critique

1. What kind of sampling strategy was used?

2. What effect does this choice of strategy have on your confidence that the results are valid?

3. Can you think of any alternative sampling strategies for this kind of research?

Study 2.   Rap music and health risk behavior. (Wingood et al., 2003)

Rap music videos are the focus of increasing attention by researchers concerned about the behavior and attitudes of young people. This study examined whether exposure to rap music videos could predict health risk behaviors and sexually transmitted diseases among African American adolescent females over a 12-month period. The study screened female teenagers residing in nonurban, lower-socioeconomic-status neighborhoods from school health classes and county health department clinics. Students were eligible if they were African American, female, between ages 14 and 18, had been sexually active in the previous six months, and provided written informed consent. The study enrolled 522 single African American females.

Yu, J., Evans, P. C., & Perfetti, L. (2003). Attitudes toward seeking treatment among alcohol-using college students. *American Journal of Drug & Alcohol Abuse, 29*(3), 671–690.

Wingood, G. M., DiClemente, R. J., Bernhardt, J. M., Harrington, K., Davies, S. L., Robillard, A., et al. (2003). A prospective study of exposure to rap music videos and African American female adolescents' health. *American Journal of Public Health, 93*(3), 437–439.

Sampling Critique

1. What kind of sampling strategy was used?

2. What effect does this choice of strategy have on your confidence that the results are valid?

3. Can you think of any alternative sampling strategies for this kind of research?

Study 3.   The mental health of adults in Iran. (Noorbala, Bagheri Yazdi, Yasamy, & Mohammad, 2004)

The prevalence of mental disorders in Iran is currently unknown. This study sought to determine the mental health status of a population sample aged 15 years and over. A sample of 35,014 individuals was selected by random cluster sampling. Participants completed the 28-item version of the General Health Questionnaire. A semi-structured clinical interview was also included to gather data on learning disability, epilepsy and psychosis. The study results indicated that about a fifth of the people in the study (25.9 percent of the women and 14.9 percent of the men) were diagnosable. The study included a number of analyses showing that there are wide regional differences and women are at greater risk.

Sampling Critique

1. What kind of sampling strategy was used?

2. What effect does this choice of strategy have on your confidence that the results are valid?

3. Can you think of any alternative sampling strategies for this kind of research?

Noorbala, A. A., Bagheri Yazdi, S. A., Yasamy, M. T., & Mohammad, K. (2004). Mental health survey of the adult population in Iran. *British Journal of Psychiatry January, 184,* 70–73.

Study 4.   Internet use and mental health. (Mathy & Cooper, 2003)

Prior research has noted that Internet usage may increase communication but decrease social involvement. This study examined the relationship between duration and frequency of Internet usage and five mental health domains. A community-based sample of 40,935 Internet users was obtained via the website of a major news organization. Every 1,000th visitor to the news organization's website was invited to participate in a study of human sexuality, resulting in a sample of 7,544 participants. Analyses revealed that duration mediated the adverse effects of frequency in some domains and that age was significantly associated with adverse outcomes of Internet use.

Sampling Critique

1. What kind of sampling strategy was used?

2. What effect does this choice of strategy have on your confidence that the results are valid?

3. Can you think of any alternative sampling strategies for this kind of research?

Study 5.   Costs associated with alternative diagnostic procedures.
          (Smitten et al., 2004)

The purpose of this study was to evaluate costs of three different sentinel node biopsy (SNB) protocols compared to those of diagnostic axillary lymph node dissection (ALND). The study included 237 consecutive breast cancer patients who underwent SNB with frozen section diagnosis. The treatment procedures for the same patients were evaluated using three hypothetical scenarios: diagnostic ALND, SNB without frozen section diagnosis and SNB as day case surgery prior to the breast operation. The total hospital costs were calculated for all three procedures for each patient. The hospital costs per patient would have been 3020 Euros when using the ALND model, 4087 Euros had the frozen section not been applied and 4573 Euros using "SNB as day case surgery" model. These results suggest that SNB seems to be associated with higher hospital costs than diagnostic ALND and that the frozen section procedure is worthwhile as long as the false negative rate is under 35 percent.

Mathy, R. M., & Cooper, A. L. (2003). The duration and frequency of Internet use in a nonclinical sample: Suicidality, behavioral problems, and treatment histories. *Psychotherapy: Theory, Research, Practice, Training,* Spring/Summer, *40*(1–2), 125–135.

Smitten, R., Sintonen, K., Kotom, H., Krogerus, T., Lepp, L., & Leidenius, E. (2004). The impact of sentinel node biopsy and axillary staging strategy on hospital costs. *Annals of Oncology, 15,* 88–94.

Sampling Critique

1. What kind of sampling strategy was used?

2. What effect does this choice of strategy have on your confidence that the results are valid?

3. Can you think of any alternative sampling strategies for this kind of research?

Exercise 2-3b Determining the Number of Participants

In addition to considering who to include in a study and how to conduct your sampling of the participants, you have to decide how many people to include. You also must take into account practical and statistical considerations in this part of planning a study.

The practical considerations involve determining who you have access to, how you might recruit them, how you will attend to their rights as study participants, how you will reward them for helping you, and how you will handle any other follow-up contact that might be needed. Many studies have been planned with high hopes and ultimately been conducted with a sample of convenience, quite often students. Sometimes using a student sample is justifiable on scientific grounds; sometimes it is just convenient. Perhaps you have participated in such a study or are even planning one at this moment!

The statistical considerations in this part of research design are somewhat complex and in part have to do with topics you will not learn about until later in *Research Methods: The Concise Knowledge Base*. However, one major idea in this area is included in Chapter 2, "Sampling": sampling error and the standard error. The basic idea is very simple: The larger the sample, the smaller the error of measurement. This should make sense: The more members of the population you include, the less likely it is that your estimates will be wrong. Let's look at a basic example using real data from a national study of drinking, drugs, sex, and violence (bet we got your attention now!).

For this example we'll put your tax money to work by using the results of a national survey of risk behavior of high school students. This data is available, along with complete documentation, from the Centers for Disease Control website at http://www.cdc.gov/nccdphp/dash/yrbs/. Since you are studying sampling, a trip to this website would be quite informative because the survey method is sophisticated and very well described. In addition, you can download the dataset in several different formats and conduct your own analysis.

In brief, this is a school-based national survey of 9th–12th graders in the United States. The survey design was a three-stage cluster sampling strategy including procedures that attended to population density and inclusion of minority students. The particular dataset we'll use was collected in 2001 and included 150 schools and 13,601 participating students. The response rate for the schools invited to participate was 75 percent and the response rate for students was 83 percent. The survey included questions about all sorts of health behavior, from seat belts to substance use. In this example, we want to make a point about standard error, so we'll just use a little bit of this large dataset.

One of the items in the survey is the height of the student. This variable was recorded in meters in the dataset but converted to feet for this example (by dividing height in meters by .3048). First, we'll examine the entire sample and then look at how the accuracy of our estimate of student height is related to sample size by taking random subsamples of different sizes.

Figure 2-1 shows a histogram of the entire sample. For the whole group, the mean is 5.56 feet, with a standard deviation of .33. The standard error of the mean is approximately .003. This means that our 95 percent confidence interval (the mean +/– twice the standard error) would be from 5.55 to 5.57 feet. So our estimate of the average height of students is very accurate, and we can have great confidence that the average height of an American high school student is very close to 5 feet, 7 inches. Put another way, we could bet with 95 percent confidence that the true population value is about one tenth of an inch from this value. Now let's see what happens to the precision of our estimate with smaller samples.

We drew a random sample of 25 percent of the data for the next look at standard error. In Figure 2-2, you can see that reducing the sample size to one quarter of the original had no effect on our estimate of the mean or standard deviation. The standard error of the mean became .006 feet, still quite small.

Now we'll reduce the sample size again, this time to 5 percent of the original cases. In Figure 2-3, you can see the plot of the resulting 630 students included in the random sample. You'll see that the distribution still looks the same, and the estimate of the mean is very similar to the larger samples.

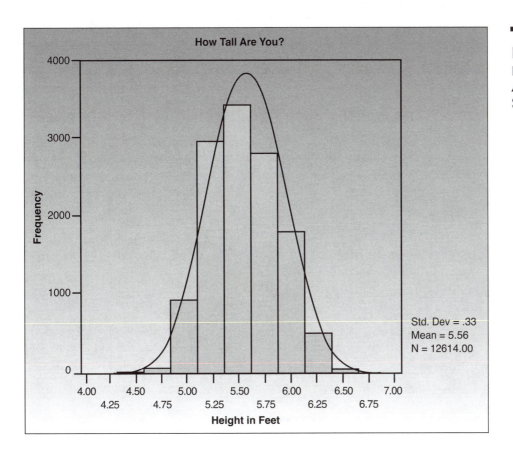

FIGURE 2-1
Estimated Height of American High School Students (N=12,614)

We'll move the sample size down again to about the level of a single classroom and take a sample of 23 cases, as shown in Figure 2-4. The estimate of the mean is 5.63 with a standard deviation of .34, still quite similar to the large sample estimate. However, the

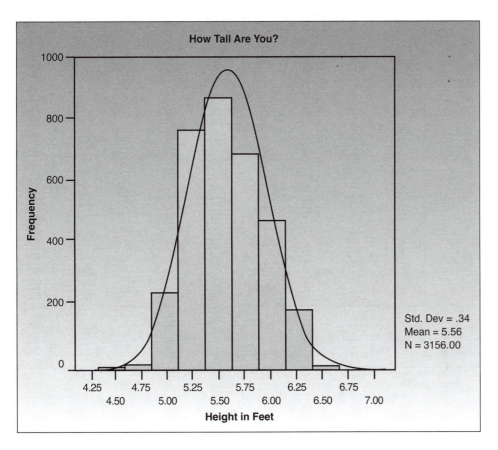

FIGURE 2-2
Height of Students (25% random sample of survey of American high school students)

FIGURE 2-3
Height of Students (5%
random sample of survey
of American high school
students)

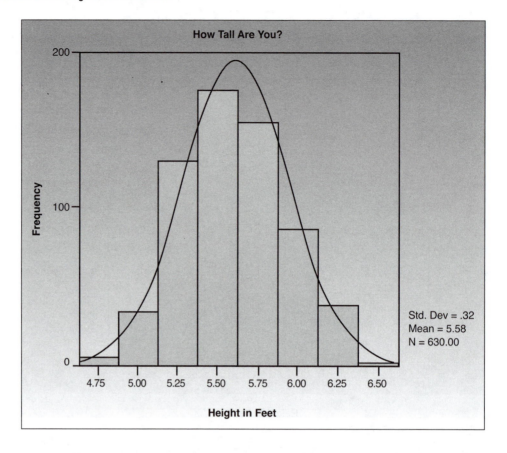

FIGURE 2-4
Height of Students (random
sample of 23 from the
survey of American high
school students)

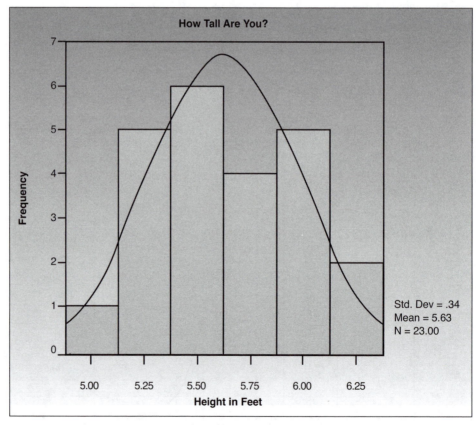

Sample	N	Mean	SD	SEM	95% CI
All students	12614	5.56	.33	.003	5.55–5.57
25% sample	3156	5.56	.34	.006	
5% sample	630	5.58	.32	.013	
Single class	23	5.63	.34	.070	

lower precision of this estimate is evident in the larger standard error of the mean, which has now become .07 feet. In case you are curious about what might happen if we take this sample even further, we did! A random sample of five cases from the entire group produced a mean of 5.71 with a standard deviation of .36. The precision (standard error) of the estimate went from .003 to .16 feet, which is about two inches.

In Table 2-1 the results are summarized, but not completely. Your job is to complete the table by figuring out and entering the 95 percent confidence intervals. As you learned in Chapter 2, "Sampling," the 95 percent confidence interval is the lower and upper bounds of our estimate based on the measurement error. That is, the confidence interval is the mean plus or minus twice the standard error. This is exactly the same thing that you have heard in countless news reports of surveys when you are told that the "margin of error is three points" (or whatever it happens to be).

Another way to think about sample size and accuracy of estimate is to plot some data showing how the number in the sample is related to the standard error of estimate. In Figure 2-5 you can see such a plot. This data was calculated by taking different size random samples from the youth risk behavior survey. You should be able to see that as sample size goes up, standard error goes down dramatically at first and then levels off. Although this graph is based on a particular dataset, the pattern is a general one.

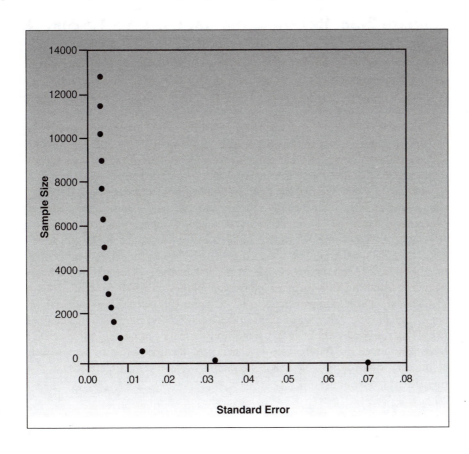

F I G U R E 2 - 5
The Relationship between Accuracy of an Estimate and Sample Size

Note: The data in this example are from the CDC national survey of high school students' health risk behavior.

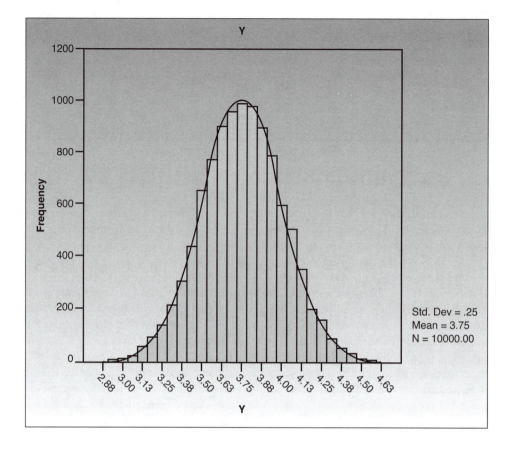

FIGURE 2-6
Histogram of the Normal Distribution of a Variable with a Mean of 3.75 and SD of .25

Exercise 2-3c Revisiting the 65, 95, & 99 Percent Rule

In this section, we'll revisit the 65, 95, & 99 percent rule with some imaginary data similar to the example in *Research Methods: The Concise Knowledge Base*. We start by generating a random sample of 10,000 normally distributed cases of a variable with a mean of 3.75 and a standard deviation of .25. In Figure 2-6, you can see the histogram of this data, which should remind you of the figures in Chapter 2, "Sampling."

In this exercise, you'll get a little bit of hands-on practice with confidence intervals and in showing yourself the relationship between sample size and measurement error. This exercise will be similar to the previous examples with the real data, except that this data is made up and you will do a little bit of the work.

In Table 2-2 you will find sample sizes listed with standard errors for the data we have been working with. Three blank columns are provided for the confidence intervals, except for the first row, where we've given you an example and a head start. To get a bit of practice in determining confidence intervals, you can apply the 65, 95, & 99 percent rule to the data and complete these columns. To review, the 65 percent boundaries are plus or minus one standard error, the 95 percent boundaries are plus or minus two standard errors, and the 99 percent boundaries are plus or minus three standard errors.

The last skill-building exercise in this chapter will be to fill in a scatterplot. In Figure 2-7 you'll see a blank set of axes with Sample Size on the Y axis and Standard Error (SEM) on the X axis. In Table 2-3 you'll find the data you need to fill in the graph. We have transformed the standard errors to make them a little easier to work with by multiplying each value by 100. Now plot the sample size and standard errors and see whether the pattern looks familiar.

Sample	N	SEM	65% CI	95% CI	99% CI
1	3	.213	3.54–3.96	3.32–4.18	3.11–4.389
2	5	.207			
3	10	.229			
4	15	.045			
5	25	.048			
6	40	.041			
7	50	.038			
8	100	.025			
9	125	.023			
10	150	.021			
11	175	.020			
12	200	.019			
13	250	.016			
14	300	.015			
15	500	.011			

TABLE 2-2

Sample Size (N), Standard Error (SEM), and Confidence Intervals (Note: M = 3.75)

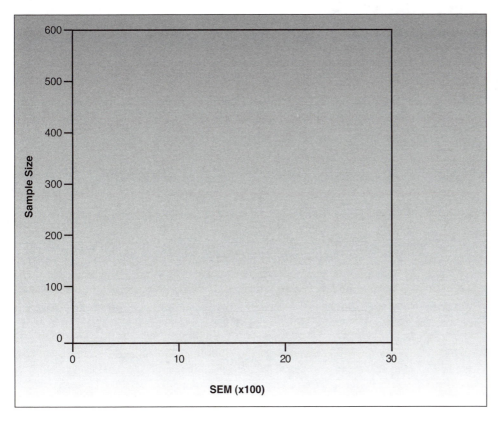

FIGURE 2-7
The Relationship between Sample Size and Standard Error of Measurement

Note: The standard error scale was multiplied by 100 to make the numbers easier to work with in this example.

TABLE 2-3	Sample	N	SEM	SEM (×100)
Sample Sizes and Standard Errors	1	3.00	.213	21.30
	2	5.00	.207	20.70
	3	10.00	.229	22.90
	4	15.00	.045	4.50
	5	25.00	.048	4.80
	6	40.00	.041	4.10
	7	50.00	.038	3.80
	8	100.00	.025	2.50
	9	125.00	.023	2.30
	10	150.00	.021	2.10
	11	175.00	.020	2.00
	12	200.00	.019	1.90
	13	250.00	.016	1.60
	14	300.00	.015	1.50
	15	500.00	.011	1.10

2-4 PRODUCTS

In considering sampling issues, your main products for planning a study will be

1. Your choice of a sampling strategy
2. Some plans about whom you might have access to
3. A plan for involving the participants that takes their specific rights into account (e.g., are they old enough to consent for themselves?)
4. Some ideas about how many participants you'll aim for

2-5 JOURNAL

In this chapter, you had practice critiquing sampling strategies and thinking about the relationship of sample size to standard error (the accuracy or precision of your measurement). The other aspect of planning sample size is called "Power analysis," a topic taken up in Chapter 11, "Analysis."

Exercise 2-5a Research Methods Sampling Self-Efficacy Evaluation

Use the following scale to rate your skills in each of the areas listed.

1 = Little or no ability to perform this task
2 = Some ability to perform this task
3 = Moderately good ability to perform this task
4 = Very good ability to perform this task
5 = Excellent ability to perform this task

1. ____Understand and use key terms in sampling.

2. ____Recognize the sampling strategies used in other research.

3. ____Identify the limits of particular sampling strategies with regard to external validity (generalizability).

4. ____Critique the sample size of research studies with regard to standard error of estimate.

5. ____Consider the consequences of sample size with regard to the accuracy of estimates you can make in your own research.

Exercise 2-5b Research Methods Sampling Self-Evaluation

In the space provided, jot down your personal reactions to Chapter 2, "Sampling," of *Research Methods: The Concise Knowledge Base*. What did you like best? What did you still need to study? How might you now improve your skills in sampling?

MEASUREMENT

The Theory
of Measurement

3-1 THE LANGUAGE OF MEASUREMENT

Exercise 3-1a The Key Terms *Preview*

Instructions. This exercise should be done before you read the chapter. Read every term in the Key Terms list. Now go back through the list again and identify up to 10 terms that you are unsure of so that you can pay special attention to them as you read. If you find that the entire list of key terms is unfamiliar, you should plan to read the chapter more than once and complete this exercise more than once as well. Write your preview terms in the following spaces:

Term 1:_____

Term 2:_____

Term 3:_____

Term 4:_____

Term 5:_____

Term 6:_____

Term 7:_____

Term 8:_____

Term 9:_____

Term 10:_____

Exercise 3-1b The Key Terms *Review*

Instructions. This exercise should be done after you read the chapter. The idea here is to see how much you've picked up to help you with the key terms you identified in your preview exercise. In the following spaces, write definitions of the terms in your own words. Try your best to do them by memory, but if you need to look them up again, go ahead and do so.

Term 1:_____ Definition:_____

_____

Term 2:_____ Definition:_____

_____

Term 3:_____ Definition:_____

_____

Term 4:_____ Definition:_____

_____

Term 5:_____ Definition:_____

_____

Term 6:_____ Definition:_____

_____

Term 7:_____ Definition:_____

_____

Term 8:_____ Definition:_____

_____

Term 9:_____ Definition:_____

_____

Term 10:_____ Definition:_____

_____

3-2 CONCEPTS

Exercise 3-2a Understanding and Communicating
Key Ideas

Instructions. This exercise can be used to help you understand passages in *Research Methods: The Concise Knowledge Base*. You will need a partner for this exercise. Ideally, your partner would be a classmate in your research methods course or an advanced student. If a classmate or other fellow student is not available, you may try the exercise with another willing person. Feel free to draw pictures or make up examples to help you explain the idea.

1. **Identify** a passage in Chapter 3, "The Theory of Measurement," of *Research Methods: The Concise Knowledge Base* that you would like to understand better. Keep in mind that if you are unsure of several parts of the chapter, do the earlier ones first because understanding the latter ones might depend on how well you understand the earlier ones.

2. **Read** the passage aloud to your partner. You may read it more than once if your partner requests you to do so.

3. **Discuss** the passage. Ask your partner to tell you what she or he heard in her or his own words. Give your partner feedback about what you think is the accuracy of her or his comment. If you discover discrepancies between your understanding and your partner's, read the passage aloud again.

4. **Write** the passage in the space provided. You and your partner should write a summary of the passage in your own words. After you have finished writing, read your passage to your partner and then allow your partner to take a turn.

5. **Conclusion.** You and your partner should now ask the question, "OK, now do we get it?" The evidence of improvement is your mutual understanding, your ability to discuss the passage orally, and your ability to write a brief summary. If you find that the passage is still unclear, well, that's what professors, email, and questions are for!

3-3 SKILLS

The primary skills that researchers need in quantitative kinds of measurement apply to two general kinds of situations: developing a new measure or using one that is already established. You first need to identify the constructs you want to study and then figure out whether they are measurable. We could also say that, in general, researchers begin planning their measurement strategies by reviewing the field to see what is out there. This process involves skills in locating and critiquing measures to see whether they are adequate for your study. When no good measure exists, the researcher must consider developing a new measure. As you might imagine, this is always an ambitious project in and of itself. Thorough training in measurement comes with years of study and practice. In the workbook, our goal is to introduce you to the skills needed as you enter the field and help you to plan your first study. We will practice reviewing and critiquing measures, and then do just a little bit with measure development.

Exercise 3-3a Finding Published Measures and Reviews

As noted, sometimes your task is primarily to see whether a measure already exists and then to decide if it is adequate for your study objectives. Unfortunately, you can't go to the mall and visit the "Measure Mart" (at least we haven't seen one yet). So you must do what countless other students have done: search until you have exhausted the possibilities. If you are enrolled at a college or university, you probably have access to some of the most important sources, but you can supplement your library search with a variety of other possibilities. The following is a list of common sources of measures and information about them:

- Publishers
- Specialized handbooks
- Professional/Academic reviews of measures
- Professional organizations
- Websites of measure developers or researchers
- Test authors
- Professors and other researchers (personal or email contact)
- Clinical settings where a particular issue is addressed

Now we will attempt to guide you somewhat systematically through the available resources. The first question is

*What is the construct you want to measure?*_____

If you've not settled on one construct, you should at least browse the sources listed later in this exercise to get a feel for them. Most people begin the process of searching for measures with some well-known databases available through many, if not most, libraries and via the Internet. For example, in the fields of education and psychology, there are several such sources, including the following. In this exercise, your task is to identify a construct and then to search the possible sources of an existing measure, recording the results of your search here in the workbook. You may have identified more than one construct that you want to include in your study, but we'll start with one, and you may repeat the process as needed.

1. *The Buros Institute of Mental Measurements.* (http://www.unl.edu/buros/)

    The Buros Institute publishes three important sources of information related to published measures, including *Mental Measurements Yearbook, Tests In Print,* and *Test Reviews Online.* The yearbook provides reviews of more than 2,000 measures. These reviews are written by one or two experts in the field. *Test Reviews Online* includes these same reviews in an electronic database. The *Tests In Print* volume is a comprehensive bibliography of all known commercially available tests in English. If your library does not have a license for these reviews, you can purchase an individual review (the current cost is $15).

    Record Your Search Results Here (include such things as the number of hits, the availability of reviews, access to the tests, and other information to help you in your search).

2. *The Educational Testing Service Test Locator* (http://www.ets.org/testcoll/)

   The ETS Test database contains information on more than 20,000 measures and is the largest in the world. It was created specifically for you! (OK, and all the other researchers in the world.) You can search the database by test name or acronym, keyword, author, publisher, year, and other descriptors. You can also find out about the availability of the test.

   Search Results (include such things as the number of hits, the availability of reviews, access to the tests, and other information to help you in your search).

3. *Health and Psychosocial Instruments (HAPI)* (You'll have to access this one through your library system).

   This library-based database provides access to information measures used in the health fields, psychosocial sciences, organizational behavior, and library and information science. A search of this database will lead you to published sources that have used the measure. Some of them will be sources that are complete with information about the measure's reliability and validity, but some provide only a limited description of the measure.

   Search Results (include such things as the number of hits, the availability of reviews, access to the tests, and other information to help you in your search).

4. *Handbooks and Compendia*

A rather large number of handbooks and compendia of measures is also available for purchase or can be borrowed from your library. The advantage of using such a source is that you will usually get complete test development information, including reliability and validity data. Most often you'll also find out about costs and access to the measure as well as some evaluation of it. And in some cases, you may obtain all you need directly from the book, including the legal right to use it in research, the test items, and instructions for scoring and interpretation. Listing all the handbooks available would be impossible, but you might begin by searching your library catalog and then book distributors on the Internet. (Scarily, when I entered the term "handbook of measures" in Google, it returned more than 1.5 million hits! So please be specific when you search the web [i.e., include some keywords related to your construct].)

Search Results (include such things as the number of hits, the availability of reviews, access to the tests, and other information to help you in your search).

Exercise 3-3b Practice in Measurement Critique

In this exercise, we'll review some imaginary measures and critique them in terms of the validity and reliability ideas in Chapter 3, "The Theory of Measurement." First, you'll read a description of the construct and measure and then be asked to respond to a series of critical questions about the measure.

Construct: Quality of Virtual Life

Quality of life is a construct that is relevant to many fields. Public policy analysts, sociologists, and economists want to measure it at the level of the community, state, or nation. Physicians, nurses, and patients want to pay attention to quality of life in medical treatment. Psychologists and psychiatrists want to understand it at both of these levels and in terms of the individual's experience. People seem to agree that it is important but are not exactly in agreement about how to define or measure the construct. One area that no one has yet explored is quality of life when life is experienced virtually via the computer.

   Background: The technology revolution continues to affect all aspects of life. In 2004, people order pizzas; find jobs; play games; take courses; buy cars; search for marital prospects; download music; maintain relationships via email, chat rooms, and instant messaging; and so on, and so on, and so on. The pace of change and unquestioned acceptance of these changes might be assumed to enhance one's quality of life. Yet questions could be raised about cost, environmental, physical, psychological, and other consequences of the technology revolution. For this exercise, we will define quality of virtual life as including any aspect of life that has (or had) a physical analog or counterpart. That is, anything that can be done on the computer is "virtual" and done physically is "real" life.

Measurement Objective: A Valid and Reliable Measure of Quality of Virtual Life

Measurement Development Strategies and Critique: Now you'll read descriptions of how three researchers approached this problem and will be asked to critically review each one.

Case 1. The E-QoL-1 (a measure of electronic quality of life)

Description of Measure: Professor Smart realized that she had extensive experience with online communication because of her work at her college. She also realized that this experience was common among her colleagues and decided that she could tap their expertise in developing her measure of electronic quality of life. Her method was to invite a select group of 10 of her colleagues to a discussion board that she set up on her website. She posed this question: How has electronic communication affected your quality of life? She monitored and encouraged the discussion for four weeks and then downloaded the entire discussion. She then coded the discussion for key statements and turned each idea into an item for a measure. When she had finished, she had 30 items and was ready to validate the measure. To accomplish this task, she emailed the measure to the 10 colleagues from the discussion board and asked them to carefully review the items. She asked them to give her feedback on whether the measure appeared to represent the quality of their electronic life. After she had heard back from them, she revised the items appropriately, pronounced the measure valid, and began to plan a study with the measure.

Sampling

1. What kind of validity do you think this measure possesses, if any? Why do you think so?

2. Do you see any major weaknesses in the validity of the measure?

3. What is the impact of the sampling strategy used?

4. What next steps could you suggest for Professor Smart to add to her validation of the measure?

5. Discuss what steps the professor could take to examine the reliability of her measure.

Case 2. The E-QoL-2 (another measure of electronic quality of life)

Description of Measure: Professor Smarter read the article about the new measure of electronic quality of life (the E-QoL-1) and decided that he could do better. His strategy was as follows. He first recruited 250 students from the psychology department volunteer pool to participate in the study. He conducted his study in two stages. The first stage was to have the students keep a daily diary of electronic activities for one week so he could have an inventory of what the students did, how much they did it, and what their reflections were on how it affected them. Next, he coded all the activities into categories with examples from the diaries. He also examined how frequently each activity was done and eliminated the ones that rarely occurred to keep the list manageable. The next step was to review and code all the things that the students said were consequences of their electronic activities. Again, he put them into categories and ended up with five dimensions: relationships, health, productivity, finances, and recreation. Finally, he put it all together. The measure had a list of 15 activities with ratings of the impact on all five dimensions. To validate the measure, he had all 250 of the students complete it along with a previously validated general quality of life measure. He examined the correlations between his new measure and the other quality of life measure. He also calculated the internal consistency reliability (Cronbach's Coefficient Alpha), and the test-retest reliability by giving the E-QoL-2 measure to the students a second time one month after they had taken it the first time.

Sampling

1. What kind of validity do you think this measure possesses, if any? Why do you think so?

2. Do you see any major weaknesses in the validity of the measure?

3. What is the impact of the sampling strategy used?

4. What next steps could you suggest for Professor Smarter to add to his validation of the measure?

5. Discuss what other steps the professor could take to examine the reliability of his measure.

Case 3. The E-QoL-3 (Your measure!)

Design your own measure of electronic quality of life. In the space provided, outline the steps that you could take to extend this line of research even further. Try to think of the strengths as well as the weaknesses of the two examples you've critiqued and see whether you can think of ways of adding to the validity and reliability of such a measure. (An alternative exercise would be to use this portion of the workbook to outline the steps needed to develop your own measure of the construct you are planning to study. This information would be especially useful if you've discovered that there are no existing measures for your study.)

3-4 PRODUCTS

In considering measurement issues, your main products for planning a study will be

1. Identification of the constructs for your study

2. A list of previously published measures of this construct along with any available reviews and information about the availability of the measure

3. Some decisions about whether the existing measures are adequate in terms of validity and reliability; appropriate for your population; and feasible because of cost, training, or other considerations

4. If necessary, an alternative plan for developing your own measure

3-5 JOURNAL

In this chapter, you had practice critiquing measurement strategies and thinking about ways of studying the validity and reliability of a measure. Most students at the graduate level and many undergraduates will complete an entire course in measurement in which these skills can be practiced again. The greatest practice probably comes from attempting to construct your own measure. To complete the chapter, do the self-evaluation that follows.

Exercise 3-5a Research Methods Measurement Self-Efficacy Evaluation

Use the following scale to rate your skills in each of the areas listed.

1 = Little or no ability to perform this task
2 = Some ability to perform this task
3 = Moderately good ability to perform this task
4 = Very good ability to perform this task
5 = Excellent ability to perform this task

1. ____Understand and use key terms in measurement.

2. ____Identify a construct that could be measured.

3. ____Locate an existing measure of your construct.

4. ____Critique an existing measure of a construct.

5. ____Outline steps that could be taken to develop a new measure with awareness of the strengths and weaknesses of your approach with regard to reliability and validity.

Exercise 3-5b Research Methods Measurement
Self-Evaluation

In the space provided, jot down your personal reactions to Chapter 3, "The Theory of Measurement," of *Research Methods: The Concise Knowledge Base*. What did you like best? What did you still need to study? How might you now improve your skills in measurement?

4

Survey Research

Chapter Outline

4-1 THE LANGUAGE OF SURVEY RESEARCH

Exercise 4-1a The Key Terms *Preview*

Instructions. This exercise should be done before you read the chapter. Read every term in the Key Terms list. Now go back through the list again and identify up to 10 terms that you are unsure of so that you can pay special attention to them as you read. If you find that the entire list of key terms is unfamiliar, you should plan to read the chapter more than once and complete this exercise more than once as well. Write your preview terms in the following spaces:

Term 1:_____

Term 2:_____

Term 3:_____

Term 4:_____

Term 5:_____

Term 6:_____

Term 7:_____

Term 8:_____

Term 9:_____

Term 10:_____

Exercise 4-1b The Key Terms *Review*

Instructions. This exercise should be done after you read the chapter. The idea here is to see how much you've picked up to help you with the key terms you identified in your preview exercise. In the following spaces, write definitions of the terms in your own words. Try your best to do them by memory, but if you need to look them up again, go ahead and do so.

Term 1:_____ Definition:_____

_____

Term 2:_____ Definition:_____

_____

Term 3:_____ Definition:_____

_____

Term 4:_____ Definition:_____

_____

Term 5:_____ Definition:_____

_____

Term 6:_____ Definition:_____

_____

Term 7:_____ Definition:_____

_____

Term 8:_____ Definition:_____

_____

Term 9:_____ Definition:_____

_____

Term 10:_____ Definition:_____

_____

4-2 CONCEPTS

Exercise 4-2a Understanding and Communicating Key Ideas

Instructions. This exercise can be used to help you understand passages in *Research Methods: The Concise Knowledge Base*. You will need a partner for this exercise. Ideally, your partner would be a classmate in your research methods course or an advanced student. If a classmate or other fellow student is not available, you may try the exercise with another willing person. Feel free to draw pictures or make up examples to help you explain the idea.

1. **Identify** a passage in Chapter 4, "Survey Research," of *Research Methods: The Concise Knowledge Base* that you would like to understand better. Keep in mind that if you are unsure of several parts of the chapter, do the earlier ones first because understanding the latter ones might depend on how well you understand the earlier ones.

2. **Read** the passage aloud to your partner. You may read it more than once if your partner requests you to do so.

3. **Discuss** the passage. Ask your partner to tell you what she or he heard in her or his own words. Give your partner feedback about what you think is the accuracy of her or his comment. If you discover discrepancies between your understanding and your partner's, read the passage aloud again.

4. **Write** the passage in the space provided. You and your partner should write a summary of the passage in your own words. After you have finished writing, read your passage to your partner and then allow your partner to take a turn.

5. **Conclusion.** You and your partner should now ask the question, "OK, now do we get it?" The evidence of improvement is your mutual understanding, your ability to discuss the passage orally, and your ability to write a brief summary. If you find that the passage is still unclear, well, that's what professors, email, and questions are for!

4-3 SKILLS

In this chapter, we'll continue to work on survey research skills by working with survey items.

Exercise 4-3a Recognition of Item Formats

In this exercise, you'll see a set of items from *Research Methods: The Concise Knowledge Base* (or slight adaptations of them). They are reordered to allow you to check your retention of the differences between the various kinds of items. Your task for this exercise is to identify the *type* of item from the list provided.

Item Types

A. Dichotomous
B. Nominal-level
C. Ordinal-level
D. Interval-level
E. Semantic Differential
F. Cumulative Response
G. Filter or Contingency
H. Unstructured or open-ended

1. Please check each statement that you agree with:

    ____ Are you willing to permit immigrants to live in your country?

    ____ Are you willing to permit immigrants to live in your community?

    ____ Are you willing to permit immigrants to live in your neighborhood?

    ____ Would you be willing to have an immigrant live next door to you?

    ____ Would you let your child marry an immigrant?

    What type of item is this?_____

2. What is your occupational field?

    ____ Business

    ____ Education

    ____ Health Care

    ____ Government

    ____ Other

    What type of item is this?_____

3. The death penalty is justifiable under some circumstances.

1	2	3	4	5
strongly disagree	disagree	neutral	agree	strongly agree

    What type of item is this?_____

4. Have you ever smoked marijuana?

___ Yes

___ No

If yes, about how many times have you smoked marijuana?

___ Once

___ 2 to 5 times

___ 6 to 10 times

___ 11 to 20 times

___ more than 20 times

What type of item is this?_____

5. Rank the candidates in order of preference from best to worst:

___ George Bush

___ John Kerry

___ Dennis Kucinich

___ Al Sharpton

___ Ralph Nader

What type of item is this?_____

6. Do you believe that the death penalty is ever justified?

___ Yes

___ No

What type of item is this?_____

7. Do you have any other comments?

What type of item is this?_____

Exercise 4-3b Practice in Sequencing of Items

In this exercise, you'll have a chance to consider the issues involved in proper sequencing of survey items. Read all the items listed here and then place a number in the blank to indicate what you think the correct placement in the survey should be.

   1. Place the item sequence number in the blank.

       _____ Do you think the death penalty is ever justified?

       _____ What is your age?

       _____ Have you or any member of your family been a victim of a violent crime?

       _____ Are you registered with a political party, and if so, which one?

       _____ Did you vote in the last presidential election?

   2. Place the item sequence number in the blank.

       _____ Have any children in your household had an asthma attack in the past year?

       _____ What are the first names and ages of the children in your household?

       _____ Is there a member of your family available who could answer questions about the children's health?

       _____ How many asthma attacks would you say that _____ (child's name) has had in the past month?

       _____ Do any children reside in your home?

Exercise 4-3c Practice in Writing Survey Items

In this exercise, you can practice writing survey items in the various formats reviewed. If you are actually planning to conduct a survey for your study, you might use this exercise to produce the first draft of your survey.

What is the construct that you want to study in your interview (e.g., attitudes toward the government, health behavior, occupational satisfaction, etc.)?

1. Write an item on this construct utilizing a dichotomous item format.

2. Write an item on this construct utilizing a nominal-level response format.

3. Write an item on this construct utilizing an ordinal-level response format.

4. Write an item on this construct utilizing a interval-level response format.

5. Write an item on this construct utilizing a cumulative-response response format.

6. Write an item on this construct utilizing a filter or contingency question response format.

4-4 PRODUCTS

Your list of products will vary depending on what kind of study you are planning and depending on what your instructor has asked you to do. Your list may include the following:

1.   Identification of options for formatting your survey or interview items
2.   A draft of some items for your survey or interview

4-5 JOURNAL

In this chapter, you had practice considering survey and interview measurement strategies. You should now review and rate yourself on the competencies listed in the following self-evaluation.

Exercise 4-5a Research Methods Survey Research Self-Efficacy Evaluation

Use the following scale to rate your skills in each of the areas listed.

1 = Little or no ability to perform this task
2 = Some ability to perform this task
3 = Moderately good ability to perform this task
4 = Very good ability to perform this task
5 = Excellent ability to perform this task

1. ____Understand and use key terms in survey research.

2. ____Identify the types of item formats that can be used in a survey.

3. ____Write survey items according to a specified format.

Exercise 4-5b Research Methods Survey Research Self-Evaluation

In the space provided, jot down your personal reactions to Chapter 4, "Survey Research," of *Research Methods: The Concise Knowledge Base*. What did you like best? What did you still need to study? How might you now improve your skills in survey research?

5

Scales and Indexes

Chapter Outline

5-1 THE LANGUAGE OF SCALES AND INDEXES

Exercise 5-1a The Key Terms *Preview*

Instructions. This exercise should be done before you read the chapter. Read every term in the Key Terms list. Now go back through the list again and identify up to 10 terms that you are unsure of so that you can pay special attention to them as you read. If you find that the entire list of key terms is unfamiliar, you should plan to read the chapter more than once and complete this exercise more than once as well. Write your preview terms in the following spaces:

Term 1:_____

Term 2:_____

Term 3:_____

Term 4:_____

Term 5:_____

Term 6:_____

Term 7:_____

Term 8:_____

Term 9:_____

Term 10:_____

Exercise 5-1b The Key Terms *Review*

Instructions. This exercise should be done after you read the chapter. The idea here is to see how much you've picked up to help you with the key terms you identified in your preview exercise. In the following spaces, write definitions of the terms in your own words. Try your best to do them by memory, but if you need to look them up again, go ahead and do so.

Term 1:_____ Definition:_____

_____

Term 2:_____ Definition:_____

_____

Term 3:_____ Definition:_____

_____

Term 4:_____ Definition:_____

_____

Term 5:_____ Definition:_____

_____

Term 6:_____ Definition:_____

_____

Term 7:_____ Definition:_____

_____

Term 8:_____ Definition:_____

_____

Term 9:_____ Definition:_____

_____

Term 10:_____ Definition:_____

_____

5-2 CONCEPTS

Exercise 5-2a Understanding and Communicating Key Ideas

Instructions. This exercise can be used to help you understand passages in *Research Methods: The Concise Knowledge Base*. You will need a partner for this exercise. Ideally, your partner would be a classmate in your research methods course or an advanced student. If a classmate or other fellow student is not available, you may try the exercise with another willing person. Feel free to draw pictures or make up examples to help you explain the idea.

1. **Identify** a passage in Chapter 5, "Scales and Indexes," of *Research Methods: The Concise Knowledge Base* that you would like to understand better. Keep in mind that if you are unsure of several parts of the chapter, do the earlier ones first because understanding the latter ones might depend on how well you understand the earlier ones.

2. **Read** the passage aloud to your partner. You may read it more than once if your partner requests you to do so.

3. **Discuss** the passage. Ask your partner to tell you what she or he heard in her or his own words. Give your partner feedback about what you think is the accuracy of her or his comment. If you discover discrepancies between your understanding and your partner's, read the passage aloud again.

4. **Write** the passage in the space provided. You and your partner should write a summary of the passage in your own words. After you have finished writing, read your passage to your partner and then allow your partner to take a turn.

5. **Conclusion.** You and your partner should now ask the question, "OK, now do we get it?" The evidence of improvement is your mutual understanding, your ability to discuss the passage orally, and your ability to write a brief summary. If you find that the passage is still unclear, well, that's what professors, email, and questions are for!

5-3 SKILLS

In this chapter, you moved a step beyond survey research to learn how indexes and scales can be constructed. As in *Research Methods: The Concise Knowledge Base,* we'll practice using indexes first and then scales.

Exercise 5-3a Identifying the Order of Steps in Constructing an Index

Here, you can see the four steps in constructing an index. Let's begin by placing them in the proper order. Number the following steps according to the way you would do them in a study.

_____ Develop the rules for calculating the index score.

_____ Operationalize and measure the components.

_____ Conceptualize the index.

_____ Validate the index score.

Exercise 5-3b Identifying the Steps in Constructing an Index

Now we'll practice labeling the steps in the development of an index with an example. In *Research Methods: The Concise Knowledge Base*, you read about the Consumer Price Index (CPI). Let's imagine that a student researcher wanted to develop such an index for her college campus and carried out the following steps to do so. Let's call it the College Consumer Price Index (CCPI). Your job is to label the steps according to the four major operations (those you just ordered in Exercise 5-3a).

1. The student researcher wanted to check on the representativeness of the items in the CCPI, so she had a group of students (randomly identified from the student directory) complete a spending diary each day for what she thought was a typical week in the school year. All the students wrote down every item they bought and how much they paid for it. The researcher then compared the items and their costs with her index list.

    What step in developing an index was this?

    ____ Conceptualizing the index

    ____ Operationalizing and measuring the components

    ____ Developing the rules for calculating the index score

    ____ Validating the index score

2. The student researcher studied the U.S. Consumer Price Index and tried to find any previous studies about the cost of living for college students and what had been included in the previous studies. She reviewed her own expenditures over the past year and wrote them all down. Then she conducted interviews with friends and classmates about all the things they spend money on. She assembled every item from all these sources into a list. She then classified all the items into two categories: necessities and discretionary purchases (i.e., fun). She decided that her CCPI would include an overall index and then one for each of her two major categories of spending.

    What step in developing an index was this?

    ____ Conceptualizing the index

    ____ Operationalizing and measuring the components

    ____ Developing the rules for calculating the index score

    ____ Validating the index score

3. The researcher thought about the relative importance of the items on her list of college expenses and concluded that the necessities ought to count more than the discretionary items in her index. So she decided to assign a weight to the items to reflect this judgment.

    What step in developing an index was this?

    ____ Conceptualizing the index

    ____ Operationalizing and measuring the components

    ____ Developing the rules for calculating the index score

    ____ Validating the index score

4. Because she was mainly interested in the cost of living at her school, the researcher took her list of items and found the current price for each one by looking them up on the school website and visiting nearby examples of the kinds of places students listed to check the cost of things (e.g., movie theaters and restaurants near the campus). She decided that this would be an index she would collect at the mid-point of each semester.

What step in developing an index was this?

_____ Conceptualizing the index

_____ Operationalizing and measuring the components

_____ Developing the rules for calculating the index score

_____ Validating the index score

Exercise 5-3c Developing Your Own Index

In this exercise, you'll outline the steps you would need to take to develop your own index. If the study you are planning might involve the use of an index, you should use the construct you are studying. If you will not be developing your own index, you may use any construct that interests you. If you are stuck, here is a suggestion: What would be the steps in constructing an index of quality of student life on your campus? Number and list the steps in the space provided.

Step 1: Conceptualization

Step 2: Operationalization

Step 3: Calculation

Step 4: Validation

Exercise 5-3d Developing a Scale

In this exercise, you will have an opportunity to develop items that could make up a scale in your own study. Follow the steps outlined and answer each question.

1. Define the focus. No matter which scaling method you will employ, you have to begin by defining the focus of your measure. To do so, you need to answer the following questions:

a. What is the construct that you will be attempting to measure (e.g., employment self-esteem)?

b. How do you conceptualize the dimensionality of this construct (e.g., low to high, good to bad, frequent to rare, etc.)?

2. Generate some potential items. In *Research Methods: The Concise Knowledge Base*, you are advised to develop a large pool of potential items. In this exercise, we'll limit it to five items.

a. Item 1_____

b. Item 2_____

c. Item 3_____

d. Item 4_____

e. Item 5_____

3. Rate the items. In this step, you clearly can see the differences in the three unidimensional scaling methods described in *Research Methods: The Concise Knowledge Base*. For this exercise, your task is to think generally about the steps you would take by answering the following questions:

a. You will need a set of experts to provide you with some ratings on the items.

i. Who could you recruit to help you with this task?

ii. What kind of expertise do these experts have with this construct?

b. Consider what kinds of ratings you'll need for each scaling method.

i. What kinds of ratings would you need to develop a scale using Thurstone's Method of Equal-Appearing Intervals?

ii. What kinds of ratings would you need to develop a scale using Likert Scaling?

iii. What kinds of ratings would you need to develop a Guttman Scale?

4. Select items. Each of the three methods requires specific procedures for selecting items. What steps would you need to take for each method?

    i. Thurstone's Method of Equal-Appearing Intervals

    ii. Likert Scale

    iii. Guttman Scale

5. Administer and score the scale. At this stage, you are ready to collect data with your new scale. Summarize the steps you would need to take for each of the three scaling methods.

    i. Thurstone's Method of Equal-Appearing Intervals

    ii. Likert Scale

    iii. Guttman Scale

5-4 PRODUCTS

Your list of products will vary depending on what kind of study you are planning and depending on what your instructor has asked you to do. Your list may include the following:

1. A major construct or constructs that could be the subject of an index or scale construction study

2. An outline of the steps you will need to take to construct such an index or scale

3. An initial set of items for your index or scale

4. A decision about the most appropriate scaling method for your study

5-5 JOURNAL

In this chapter, you had practice considering the development of indexes and scales. You should now review and rate yourself on the competencies listed in the following self-evaluation.

Exercise 5-5a Research Methods Scales and Indexes Self-Efficacy Evaluation

Use the following scale to rate your skills in each of the areas listed.

1 = Little or no ability to perform this task
2 = Some ability to perform this task
3 = Moderately good ability to perform this task
4 = Very good ability to perform this task
5 = Excellent ability to perform this task

1. _____ Understand the key terms in index and scale construction.

2. _____ Understand the key concepts in index and scale construction.

3. _____ Identify the steps in construction of an index.

4. _____ Develop an outline of the steps you would need to take in constructing an index.

5. _____ Identify the steps in construction of the three major kinds of unidimensional scales.

6. _____ Develop an outline of the steps you would need to take in constructing a unidimensional scale.

Exercise 5-5b Research Methods Scales and Indexes Self-Evaluation

In the space provided, jot down your personal reactions to Chapter 5, "Scales and Indexes," of *Research Methods: The Concise Knowledge Base*. What did you like best? What did you still need to study? How might you now improve your skills in scales and indexes?

6

Qualitative and Unobtrusive Measures

Chapter Outline

6-1 THE LANGUAGE OF QUALITATIVE AND UNOBTRUSIVE MEASURES

Exercise 6-1a The Key Terms *Preview*

Instructions. This exercise should be done before you read the chapter. Read every term in the Key Terms list. Now go back through the list again and identify up to 10 terms that you are unsure of so that you can pay special attention to them as you read. If you find that the entire list of key terms is unfamiliar, you should plan to read the chapter more than once and complete this exercise more than once as well. Write your preview terms in the following spaces:

Term 1:_____

Term 2:_____

Term 3:_____

Term 4:_____

Term 5:_____

Term 6:_____

Term 7:_____

Term 8:_____

Term 9:_____

Term 10:_____

Exercise 6-1b The Key Terms *Review*

Instructions. This exercise should be done after you read the chapter. The idea here is to see how much you've picked up to help you with the key terms you identified in your preview exercise. In the following spaces, write definitions of the terms in your own words. Try your best to do them by memory, but if you need to look them up again, go ahead and do so.

Term 1:_____ Definition: _____

_____

Term 2:_____ Definition: _____

_____

Term 3:_____ Definition: _____

_____

Term 4:_____ Definition: _____

_____

Term 5:_____ Definition: _____

_____

Term 6:_____ Definition: _____

_____

Term 7:_____ Definition: _____

_____

Term 8:_____ Definition: _____

_____

Term 9:_____ Definition: _____

_____

Term 10: _____ Definition: _____

_____

6-2 CONCEPTS

Exercise 6-2a Understanding and Communicating Key Ideas

Instructions. This exercise can be used to help you understand passages in *Research Methods: The Concise Knowledge Base*. You will need a partner for this exercise. Ideally, your partner would be a classmate in your research methods course or an advanced student. If a classmate or other fellow student is not available, you may try the exercise with another willing person. Feel free to draw pictures or make up examples to help you explain the idea.

1. **Identify** a passage in Chapter 6, "Qualitative and Unobtrusive Measures," of *Research Methods: The Concise Knowledge Base* that you would like to understand better. Keep in mind that if you are unsure of several parts of the chapter, do the earlier ones first because understanding the latter ones might depend on how well you understand the earlier ones.

2. **Read** the passage aloud to your partner. You may read it more than once if your partner requests you to do so.

3. **Discuss** the passage. Ask your partner to tell you what she or he heard in her or his own words. Give your partner feedback about what you think is the accuracy of her or his comment. If you discover discrepancies between your understanding and your partner's, read the passage aloud again.

4. **Write** the passage in the space provided. You and your partner should write a summary of the passage in your own words. After you have finished writing, read your passage to your partner and then allow your partner to take a turn.

5. **Conclusion.** You and your partner should now ask the question, "OK, now do we get it?" The evidence of improvement is your mutual understanding, your ability to discuss the passage orally, and your ability to write a brief summary. If you find that the passage is still unclear, well, that's what professors, email, and questions are for!

6-3 SKILLS

In this chapter, you learned about methods of measurement that are rather different in practice from Chapters 4, "Survey Research," and 5, "Scales and Indexes." In the following exercise, you'll practice thinking about how a phenomenon might be studied qualitatively and choosing appropriate methods. Because there are so many possibilities, we do not advise you to think of your responses to the items in "right or wrong" terms. A critical thinking perspective on this subject would emphasize an objective consideration of the consequences of particular choices in measurement.

Exercise 6-3a The Qualitative Methods Consultant

In this exercise, you will practice thinking about qualitative and unobtrusive measurement by playing the role of consultant to researchers who would like to supplement their quantitative measures with qualitative alternatives.

Case 1. Health Risk Behavior

A researcher comes to you and describes the following research interest. "I am studying health risk behavior in young people. I did a survey of a high school and found out how frequently students say they are using alcohol and drugs, smoking, and having sex. But I don't really know why they are doing these things. I was thinking that a qualitative study might help me understand that."

In the space provided, outline your recommendations for possible qualitative measurement of this phenomenon and be sure to include some consideration of the pros and cons of the strategies you suggest. If you see any ethical issues with the strategy, list them as well.

Case 2. Perceptions of Trust between People of Different Cultures

A researcher comes to you and describes the following research interest. "I want to study how people from different cultural backgrounds learn to trust each other. We did an experimental study where we randomly assigned students to conditions in which they'd talk to someone from a different culture. The conditions varied on things like dress, language and accent, skin color, and other observable things. But I think the lab might be too contrived for this kind of thing and that the people were able to guess what we were up to. I'd like to find a way to study this more naturally, without manipulating people."

In the space provided, outline your recommendations for possible qualitative measurement of this phenomenon and be sure to include some consideration of the pros and cons of the strategies you suggest. If you see any ethical issues with the strategy, list them as well.

Case 3. Your Own Study

Now consider the constructs that you are interested in studying. Imagine that you could employ any of the qualitative methods described in *Research Methods: The Concise Knowledge Base*. In the space provided, outline some possible qualitative methods that you could use to study the phenomena you are interested in. Then consider what the trade-offs might be between a qualitative and quantitative approach and summarize what you believe might be the best qualitative study of your construct.

Exercise 6-3b The Qualitative Methods Critique

In this exercise, you'll critically read the abstracts of several studies that employed qualitative methods. Following each abstract you will be asked to comment on several aspects of the study.

Study 1. Adolescent Girls' Personal Experience with Baby Think It Over Infant Simulator (Malinowski & Stamler, 2003)

Summary of the Study

This study explored adolescent girls' personal experience with an infant simulator that had to be cared for over a period of one to two weeks. This study employed the phenomenological approach. Nine adolescent high school girls were interviewed and viewed and audiotaped. Interview data was coded using a computer program. The results included three themes: (1) a parenting journey incorporating intellectual, emotive, and physical faculties; (2) recognizing the illusionary nature of previously held ideas about parenting an infant; and (3) offering counsel based on the BTIO experience. The new perspectives gained by the participants about parenting a newborn infant differed markedly from the romantic fantasies they had held prior to the experience. The teens started thinking more seriously about the consequences of sexual activity.

Study Critique

1. What did the qualitative design provide that a quantitative design would not have?

2. Comment on the study in terms of the issues of credibility, transferability, dependability, and confirmability.

Study 2. The Health Effects of Work-Based Welfare (Hildebrandt, 2002)

Summary of the Study

The purpose of this study was to identify effects of work-based welfare on the health and well-being of participants. The sample was 34 women who were enrolled in a work-based welfare program in a large urban community in the U.S. Midwest. The participants were interviewed in an inner-city adult education center, an inner-city church, a subsidized housing development, or homes of participants. Measures included a semi-structured interview guide, a demographic data sheet, and the General Well-being Schedule. The study found the human costs to people enrolled in work-based welfare included anxiety and depression as well as negative effects on health and well-being. The study also reported positive effects on well-being and empowerment. The findings indicate the complex interplay of the socioeconomic environment, mental and physical health, and the well-being of families, and the need for a broader societal response to poverty.

Malinowski, A. L., & Stamler, L. (2003). Adolescent girls' personal experience with Baby Think It Over infant simulator. *American Journal of Maternal Child Nursing, 28*(12), 205–211.

Hildebrandt, E. (2002). The health effects of work-based welfare. *Journal of Nursing Scholarship, 34*(4), 363–368.

Study Critique

1. What did the qualitative design provide that a quantitative design would not have?

2. Comment on the study in terms of the issues of credibility, transferability, dependability, and confirmability.

Study 3. Mutual Mistrust in the Medical Care of Drug Users: The Keys to the "Narc" Cabinet (Merrill, Rhodes, Deyo, Marlatt, & Bradley, 2002)

Summary of the Study

This study was designed to understand the often difficult relationships between illicit drug-using patients and their physicians. The main goal of the study was to identify the major issues that emerge during doctor and patient interactions. Qualitative analysis of data from direct observation of patient care interactions and interviews with drug-using patients and their physicians was carried out. Nineteen patients with recent active drug use, primarily opiate use, and their physician teams participated in the study. Results indicated physicians feared being deceived by drug-using patients. In particular, they questioned whether patients' requests for opiates to treat pain or withdrawal might result from addictive behavior rather than from "medically indicated" need. Physicians and drug-using patients in the teaching hospital setting display mutual mistrust, especially concerning opiate prescription. Physicians' fear of deception, inconsistency, and avoidance interact with patients' concerns that they are mistreated and stigmatized. Medical education should focus greater attention on addiction medicine and pain management.

Study Critique

1. What did the qualitative design provide that a quantitative design would not have?

2. Comment on the study in terms of the issues of credibility, transferability, dependability, and confirmability.

Merrill, J. O., Rhodes, L. A., Deyo, R. A., Marlatt, G., & Bradley, K. A. (2002). Mutual mistrust in the medical care of drug users: The keys to the "narc" cabinet. *Journal of General Internal Medicine, 17*(5), 327–333.

6-4 PRODUCTS

The products you've developed might include the following, depending on how heavily you will pursue qualitative or unobtrusive research methods:

1. An inventory of possible qualitative alternatives to the study of your area of interest

2. An outline of at least one qualitative strategy that you could use in your study

3. A justification for conducting or not conducting a qualitative study

6-5 JOURNAL

In this chapter, you had practice considering qualitative and unobtrusive measurement strategies. You should now review and rate yourself on the competencies listed in the following self-evaluation.

Exercise 6-5a   Research Methods Qualitative and Unobtrusive Measures Self-Efficacy Evaluation

Use the following scale to rate your skills in each of the areas listed.

1 = Little or no ability to perform this task
2 = Some ability to perform this task
3 = Moderately good ability to perform this task
4 = Very good ability to perform this task
5 = Excellent ability to perform this task

1. ____ Understand and communicate the key terms in qualitative and unobtrusive measures.

2. ____ Understand and communicate the key concepts in qualitative and unobtrusive measures.

3. ____ Identify the major approaches to qualitative and unobtrusive measurement.

4. ____ Outline a possible qualitative study in your area of interest.

Exercise 6-5b Research Methods Qualitative and Unobtrusive Measures Self-Evaluation

In the space provided, jot down your personal reactions to Chapter 6, "Qualitative and Unobtrusive Measures," of *Research Methods: The Concise Knowledge Base*. What did you like best? What did you still need to study? How might you now improve your skills in qualitative and unobtrusive measures?

7

Design

Chapter Outline

7-1 THE LANGUAGE OF DESIGN

Exercise 7-1a The Key Terms *Preview*

Instructions. This exercise should be done before you read the chapter. Read every term in the Key Terms list. Now go back through the list again and identify up to 10 terms that you are unsure of so that you can pay special attention to them as you read. If you find that the entire list of key terms is unfamiliar, you should plan to read the chapter more than once and complete this exercise more than once as well. Write your preview terms in the following spaces:

Term 1:_____

Term 2:_____

Term 3:_____

Term 4:_____

Term 5:_____

Term 6:_____

Term 7:_____

Term 8:_____

Term 9:_____

Term 10:_____

Exercise 7-1b The Key Terms *Review*

Instructions. This exercise should be done after you read the chapter. The idea here is to see how much you've picked up to help you with the key terms you identified in your preview exercise. In the following spaces, write definitions of the terms in your own words. Try your best to do them by memory, but if you need to look them up again, go ahead and do so.

Term 1:_____ Definition:_____

_____

Term 2:_____ Definition:_____

_____

Term 3:_____ Definition:_____

_____

Term 4:_____ Definition:_____

_____

Term 5:_____ Definition:_____

_____

Term 6:_____ Definition:_____

_____

Term 7:_____ Definition:_____

_____

Term 8:_____ Definition:_____

_____

Term 9:_____ Definition:_____

_____

Term 10: _____ Definition:_____

_____

7-2 CONCEPTS

Exercise 7-2a Understanding and Communicating Key Ideas

Instructions. This exercise can be used to help you understand passages in *Research Methods: The Concise Knowledge Base*. You will need a partner for this exercise. Ideally, your partner would be a classmate in your research methods course or an advanced student. If a classmate or other fellow student is not available, you may try the exercise with another willing person. Feel free to draw pictures or make up examples to help you explain the idea.

1. **Identify** a passage in Chapter 7, "Design," of *Research Methods: The Concise Knowledge Base* that you would like to understand better. Keep in mind that if you are unsure of several parts of the chapter, do the earlier ones first because understanding the latter ones might depend on how well you understand the earlier ones.

2. **Read** the passage aloud to your partner. You may read it more than once if your partner requests you to do so.

3. **Discuss** the passage. Ask your partner to tell you what she or he heard in her or his own words. Give your partner feedback about what you think is the accuracy of her or his comment. If you discover discrepancies between your understanding and your partner's, read the passage aloud again.

4. **Write** the passage in the space provided. You and your partner should write a summary of the passage in your own words. After you have finished writing, read your passage to your partner and then allow your partner to take a turn.

5. **Conclusion.** You and your partner should now ask the question, "OK, now do we get it?" The evidence of improvement is your mutual understanding, your ability to discuss the passage orally, and your ability to write a brief summary. If you find that the passage is still unclear, well, that's what professors, email, and questions are for!

7-3 SKILLS

Exercise 7-3a Critiquing Internal Validity

In this exercise, you'll read several examples of studies that utilized various designs to address a particular question. Then you'll critique the studies with regard to control or lack of control of threats to internal validity.

Study 1. Does Smoking Cause Cancer (Part 1)?

This question has been perhaps the major public health issue of the past 50 years in the United States. The question first received serious attention in 1948 when a first year medical student named Ernst Wynder witnessed the autopsy of a man who had died of lung cancer. He wondered what had caused the disease and looked into the man's life history. He discovered no obvious environmental problems (such as air pollution or work in a coal mine) but did learn that the man had smoked two packs of cigarettes each day for 30 years.

Critique

1. What kind of study would you call this?

2. Would you say that there was good evidence that smoking caused cancer from what you read?

3. What internal validity issues do you see in this study?

Study 2. Does Smoking Cause Cancer (Part 2)?

The young medical student (the future Dr. Wynder) knew he was on to something but needed stronger evidence. He and a colleague began interviewing patients with lung cancer as well as patients with other kinds of cancer. Altogether, their research group interviewed 649 patients with lung cancer and 600 comparison patients with other kinds of cancer. They asked all the patients about their smoking histories. They found that the occurrence of cancer was 40 times as great in the lung cancer group and that the risk of lung cancer was related to how much the person smoked (Wynder & Graham, 1950).

Wynder, E. L. & Graham, E. (1950). Tobacco smoking as a possible etiologic factor in bronchiogenic carcinoma: A study of 684 proven cases. *JAMA, 143,* 329–336.

Critique

1. What kind of study would you call this?

2. Would you say that there was good evidence that smoking caused cancer from what you read?

3. What internal validity issues do you see in this study?

Study 3. Does Smoking Cause Cancer (Part 3)?

As often happens in science, another researcher was interested in the same question at the same time, and he chose a different method of investigation. Dr. Richard Doll is a very well-known British physician and scientist who took another design approach to the question of smoking and cancer. Over a period of years, Doll and his colleagues interviewed a large number of physicians about their smoking behavior. Then he followed up to see which ones developed lung cancer. Overwhelmingly, the doctors who developed lung cancer were the smokers (Doll & Hill, 1950).

Critique

1. What kind of study would you call this?

2. Would you say that there was good evidence that smoking caused cancer from what you read?

3. What internal validity issues do you see in this study?

Doll, R. & Hill, A. B. (1950). Smoking and carcinoma of the lung. *British Medical Journal*, 739–748.

Exercise 7-3b Recognizing Designs

In this exercise, you'll be presented with a number of research designs described in the notation presented in *Research Methods: The Concise Knowledge Base*. Following each design, you will be asked a series of questions to show your understanding of the notation.

1. Design 1

Label the symbols in the design figure.

How many groups are studied in this design?

What would you call this design?

2. Design 2

Label the symbols in the design figure.

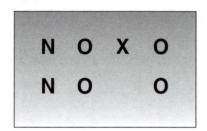

How many groups are studied in this design?

What would you call this design?

3. Design 3

Label the symbols in the design figure.

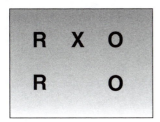

How many groups are studied in this design?

What would you call this design?

Exercise 7-3c Writing Design Notation

This exercise is similar to Exercise 7-3b except that here you'll be given the name of a design and asked to write it in notation form. Use the standard notation presented in *Research Methods: The Concise Knowledge Base*.

Design 1. Pretest–Posttest Non-Experiment

Design 2. Randomized Pretest–Posttest Experiment

Design 3. Posttest Only Non-Equivalent Groups Non-Experiment

Exercise 7-3d Writing Design Notation for Your Study and Summarizing Threats to Internal Validity

In this exercise, you'll have an opportunity to apply the design principles and ideas about internal validity to your own study. First, you'll be asked to describe the design in words and symbols and then to provide a critique of the proposed design with regard to internal validity.

1. State an hypothesis or research question.

2. Describe a study design you could use to test this hypothesis or obtain data that would inform your question.

3. Now use the design notation from *Research Methods: The Concise Knowledge Base* to describe your design.

4. Finally, review the threats to internal validity in Chapter 6, "Qualitative and Unobtrusive Measures," of *Research Methods: The Concise Knowledge Base*. What are the most significant threats to internal validity in your proposed design? Have you established control over any of the potential threats to internal validity? If so, which ones? Can you think of any ways you could modify your design to try to control threats to internal validity? Are there any ethical or practical issues you would have to consider with your alternative design?

7-4 PRODUCTS

The products from this chapter should include the following:

1. At least one possible design that you could use in your own study
2. A list of potential threats to the internal validity of your study
3. A set of alternative design possibilities to help control threats to internal validity

7-5 JOURNAL

In this chapter, you had practice considering different design strategies. You should now review and rate yourself on the competencies listed in the following self-evaluation.

Exercise 7-5a Research Methods Design Self-Efficacy Evaluation

Use the following scale to rate your skills in each of the areas listed.

1 = Little or no ability to perform this task
2 = Some ability to perform this task
3 = Moderately good ability to perform this task
4 = Very good ability to perform this task
5 = Excellent ability to perform this task

1. _____ Understand and communicate the key terms in research design and internal validity.

2. _____ Understand and communicate the key concepts in research design and its relationship to internal validity.

3. _____ Identify the components of a research design.

4. _____ Differentiate an experiment, quasi-experiment, and non-experiment on the basis of the key elements of the design.

5. _____ Recognize a research design written in notation.

6. _____ Write a research design in standard design notation.

7. _____ Identify a possible design for a research question.

8. _____ Identify the threats to the internal validity of a design proposal.

Exercise 7-5b Research Methods Design Self-Evaluation

In the space provided, jot down your personal reactions to Chapter 7, "Design," of *Research Methods: The Concise Knowledge Base*. What did you like best? What did you still need to study? How might you now improve your skills in design?

Experimental Design

Chapter Outline

8-1 THE LANGUAGE OF EXPERIMENTAL DESIGN

Exercise 8-1a The Key Terms *Preview*

Instructions. This exercise should be done before you read the chapter. Read every term in the Key Terms list. Now go back through the list again and identify up to 10 terms that you are unsure of so that you can pay special attention to them as you read. If you find that the entire list of key terms is unfamiliar, you should plan to read the chapter more than once and complete this exercise more than once as well. Write your preview terms in the following spaces:

Term 1:_____

Term 2:_____

Term 3:_____

Term 4:_____

Term 5:_____

Term 6:_____

Term 7:_____

Term 8:_____

Term 9:_____

Term 10:_____

Exercise 8-1b The Key Terms *Review*

Instructions. This exercise should be done after you read the chapter. The idea here is to see how much you've picked up to help you with the key terms you identified in your preview exercise. In the following spaces, write definitions of the terms in your own words. Try your best to do them by memory, but if you need to look them up again, go ahead and do so.

Term 1:_____ Definition:_____

_____

Term 2:_____ Definition:_____

_____

Term 3:_____ Definition:_____

_____

Term 4:_____ Definition:_____

_____

Term 5:_____ Definition:_____

_____

Term 6:_____ Definition:_____

_____

Term 7:_____ Definition:_____

_____

Term 8:_____ Definition:_____

_____

Term 9:_____ Definition:_____

_____

Term 10: _____ Definition:_____

_____

8-2 CONCPETS

Exercise 8-2a Understanding and Communicating Key Ideas

Instructions. This exercise can be used to help you understand passages in *Research Methods: The Concise Knowledge Base*. You will need a partner for this exercise. Ideally, your partner would be a classmate in your research methods course or an advanced student. If a classmate or other fellow student is not available, you may try the exercise with another willing person. Feel free to draw pictures or make up examples to help you explain the idea.

1. **Identify** a passage in Chapter 8, "Experimental Design," of *Research Methods: The Concise Knowledge Base* that you would like to understand better. Keep in mind that if you are unsure of several parts of the chapter, do the earlier ones first because understanding the latter ones might depend on how well you understand the earlier ones.

2. **Read** the passage aloud to your partner. You may read it more than once if your partner requests you to do so.

3. **Discuss** the passage. Ask your partner to tell you what she or he heard in her or his own words. Give your partner feedback about what you think is the accuracy of her or his comment. If you discover discrepancies between your understanding and your partner's, read the passage aloud again.

4. **Write** the passage in the space provided. You and your partner should write a summary of the passage in your own words. After you have finished writing, read your passage to your partner and then allow your partner to take a turn.

5. **Conclusion.** You and your partner should now ask the question, "OK, now do we get it?" The evidence of improvement is your mutual understanding, your ability to discuss the passage orally, and your ability to write a brief summary. If you find that the passage is still unclear, well, that's what professors, email, and questions are for!

8-3 SKILLS

Exercise 8-3a Identifying and Critiquing Experimental Designs

In this exercise, you will read a brief description of a study and then answer some questions about the design.

Study 1. Caffeine, Sugar, and Academic Performance

A professor was curious about the impact of student diet, especially sugar and caffeine, on test performance. She invited students from her classes to participate in a study before their mid-term exams. Forty students accepted the invitation to participate. The professor randomly assigned them to her experimental groups. The students in one group were told not to change their food or drink consumption during the week before their exams, but to record everything they ate and drank in a diary. The students in the second group were also asked to record their nutritional intake in the same kind of diary, but were also given unlimited free coffee at the campus coffee shop. The students in the third group received both free coffee and free donuts at the coffee shop, and again were asked to record everything they ate and drank. The professor planned to use the average of their mid-term grades as the dependent variable.

1. How would you label the design of this study? (Use words and symbolic notation.)

2. Were the groups equivalent at the onset of the study? How do you know?

3. Are any threats to the internal validity of the study apparent to you? If so, which threats do you see, and how might they affect the study results? Can you think of any alternative designs to address the same research question and increase control of the internal validity threats?

Exercise 8-3b Interpreting Factorial Designs

In this exercise, you'll have an opportunity to check your understanding of the use of factorial designs. We'll use the example of the educational program. As you recall, this was a study to determine which type of instruction works best. Two factors were involved: (1) the setting—in or out of class—and (2) the amount of instruction—1 versus 4 hours per week. The dependent variable was performance on a measure of learning. In *Research Methods: The Concise Knowledge Base*, you were presented with several possible alternative outcomes of the study. The basic design is reprinted here:

The 2 X 2 Design

R X_{11} O
R X_{12} O
R X_{21} O
R X_{22} O

Factor 1:   Time in Instruction

          Level 1:   1 hour per week
          Level 2:   4 hours per week

Factor 2:   Setting

          Level 1:   In-class
          Level 2:   Pull-out

First, answer the following questions to check your understanding of the design.

1. What would you call this design?

2. How many independent variables are involved in this study?

3. What are they?

4. How many levels does each independent variable have?

5. What are the levels for each independent variable?

6. What hypotheses can you test with this design?

Exercise 8-3c Understanding the Results of Factorial Design Experiments

In this exercise, you'll review the results of some studies that used a factorial design and practice interpreting the results.

Examine the data in Table 8-1 and then answer the questions that follow.

TABLE 8-1					

Factorial Design Experiment Data

Setting		Time			
		1 hr	4 hrs		
	Out	5	7	6	
	In	5	7	6	
		5	7		

1. How many independent variables are included in the table?

2. How many levels does each independent variable have?

3. What was the average score of the group that had in-class instruction for 1 hour? Circle the box (cell) in the table that shows this amount.

4. What was the average score of the group that had out-of-class instruction for 1 hour? Circle the box (cell) in the table that shows this amount.

5. What was the average score of the group that had 4 hours of instruction in the out-of-class condition? Circle the box (cell) in the table that shows this amount.

8-4 PRODUCTS

The products from this chapter should include the following:

1. At least one possible design that you could use in your own study
2. A list of potential threats to the internal validity of your study
3. A set of alternative design possibilities to help control threats to internal validity

8-5 JOURNAL

In this chapter, you had practice considering experimental design strategies. You should now review and rate yourself on the competencies listed in the following self-evaluation.

Exercise 8-5a Research Methods Experimental Design Self-Efficacy Evaluation

Use the following scale to rate your skills in each of the areas listed.

1 = Little or no ability to perform this task
2 = Some ability to perform this task
3 = Moderately good ability to perform this task
4 = Very good ability to perform this task
5 = Excellent ability to perform this task

1. _____ Understand and communicate the key terms in research design and internal validity.

2. _____ Understand and communicate the key concepts in research design and its relationship to internal validity.

3. _____ Identify the components of a research design.

4. _____ Differentiate an experiment, quasi-experiment, and non-experiment on the basis of the key elements of the design.

5. _____ Recognize a research design written in notation.

6. _____ Write a research design in standard design notation.

7. _____ Identify a possible design for a research question.

8. _____ Identify the threats to the internal validity of a design proposal.

Exercise 8-5b Research Methods Experimental Design Self-Evaluation

In the space provided, jot down your personal reactions to Chapter 8, "Experimental Design," of *Research Methods: The Concise Knowledge Base*. What did you like best? What did you still need to study? How might you now improve your skills in experimental design?

Quasi-Experimental Design

Chapter Outline

9-1 THE LANGUAGE OF QUASI-EXPERIMENTAL DESIGN

Exercise 9-1a The Key Terms *Preview*

Instructions. This exercise should be done before you read the chapter. Read every term in the Key Terms list. Now go back through the list again and identify up to 10 terms that you are unsure of so that you can pay special attention to them as you read. If you find that the entire list of key terms is unfamiliar, you should plan to read the chapter more than once and complete this exercise more than once as well. Write your preview terms in the following spaces:

Term 1:_____

Term 2:_____

Term 3:_____

Term 4:_____

Term 5:_____

Term 6:_____

Term 7:_____

Term 8:_____

Term 9:_____

Term 10:_____

Exercise 9-2b The Key Terms *Review*

Instructions. This exercise should be done after you read the chapter. The idea here is to see how much you've picked up to help you with the key terms you identified in your preview exercise. In the following spaces, write definitions of the terms in your own words. Try your best to do them by memory, but if you need to look them up again, go ahead and do so.

Term 1:_____ Definition: _____

_____

Term 2:_____ Definition: _____

_____

Term 3:_____ Definition: _____

_____

Term 4:_____ Definition: _____

_____

Term 5:_____ Definition: _____

_____

Term 6:_____ Definition: _____

_____

Term 7:_____ Definition: _____

_____

Term 8:_____ Definition: _____

_____

Term 9:_____ Definition: _____

_____

Term 10: _____ Definition: _____

_____

9-2 CONCEPTS

Exercise 9-2a Understanding and Communicating Key Ideas

Instructions. This exercise can be used to help you understand passages in *Research Methods: The Concise Knowledge Base*. You will need a partner for this exercise. Ideally, your partner would be a classmate in your research methods course or an advanced student. If a classmate or other fellow student is not available, you may try the exercise with another willing person. Feel free to draw pictures or make up examples to help you explain the idea.

1. **Identify** a passage in Chapter 9, "Quasi-Experimental Design," of *Research Methods: The Concise Knowledge Base* that you would like to understand better. Keep in mind that if you are unsure of several parts of the chapter, do the earlier ones first because understanding the latter ones might depend on how well you understand the earlier ones.

2. **Read** the passage aloud to your partner. You may read it more than once if your partner requests you to do so.

3. **Discuss** the passage. Ask your partner to tell you what she or he heard in her or his own words. Give your partner feedback about what you think is the accuracy of her or his comment. If you discover discrepancies between your understanding and your partner's, read the passage aloud again.

4. **Write** the passage in the space provided. You and your partner should write a summary of the passage in your own words. After you have finished writing, read your passage to your partner and then allow your partner to take a turn.

5. **Conclusion.** You and your partner should now ask the question, "OK, now do we get it?" The evidence of improvement is your mutual understanding, your ability to discuss the passage orally, and your ability to write a brief summary. If you find that the passage is still unclear, well, that's what professors, email, and questions are for!

9-3 SKILLS

Exercise 9-3a Identifying and Understanding Outcomes of Quasi-Experimental Designs

Instructions. In the graphs shown in Figures 9-1 through 9-6, you'll see the possible outcomes of a non-equivalent groups design. The questions that follow will provide practice in interpretation of results, especially with regard to internal validity concerns.

Quasi-Experimental Design Outcome 1

FIGURE 9-1
Plot of Pretest and Posttest Means for Possible Outcome 1

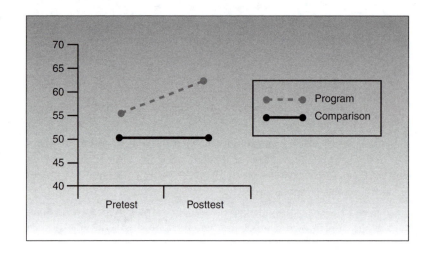

1. How would you interpret the graph (i.e., what happened in the two groups from pre- to posttest)?

2. What are the alternative explanations for the outcome observed? Which threats to validity are most likely to influence the results?

Quasi-Experimental Design Outcome 2

FIGURE 9-2
Plot of Pretest and Posttest Means for Possible Outcome 2

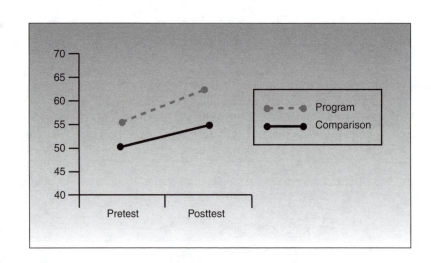

1. How would you interpret the graph (i.e., what happened in the two groups from pre- to posttest)?

2. What are the alternative explanations for the outcome observed? Which threats to validity are most likely to influence the results?

Quasi-Experimental Design Outcome 3

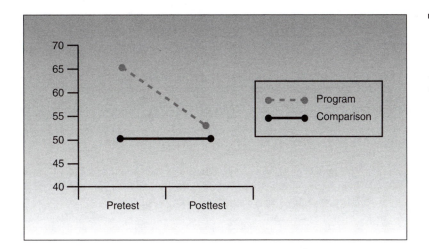

FIGURE 9-3
Plot of Pretest and Posttest Means for Possible Outcome 3

1. How would you interpret the graph (i.e., what happened in the two groups from pre- to posttest)?

2. What are the alternative explanations for the outcome observed? Which threats to validity are most likely to influence the results?

Quasi-Experimental Design Outcome 4

FIGURE 9-4
**Plot of Pretest and Posttest
Means for Possible
Outcome 4**

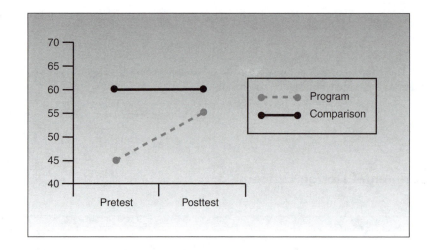

1. How would you interpret the graph (i.e., what happened in the two groups from pre- to posttest)?

2. What are the alternative explanations for the outcome observed? Which threats to validity are most likely to influence the results?

Quasi-Experimental Design Outcome 5

FIGURE 9-5
**Plot of Pretest and Posttest
Means for Possible
Outcome 5**

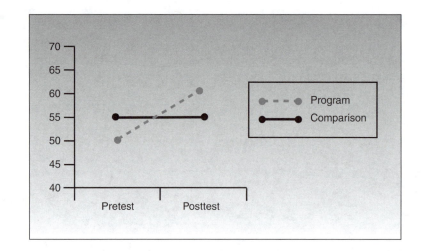

1. How would you interpret the graph (i.e., what happened in the two groups from pre- to posttest)?

2. What are the alternative explanations for the outcome observed? Which threats to validity are most likely to influence the results?

Regression-Discontinuity Design Outcomes

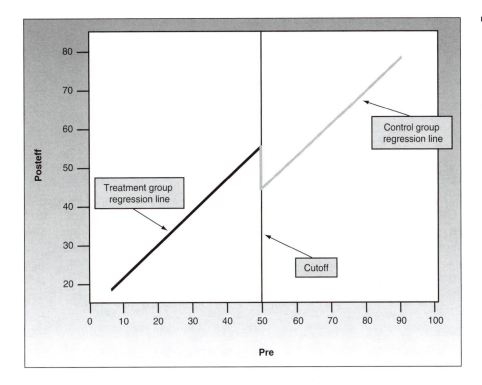

FIGURE 9-6
Regression Lines for the Data Shown in Figure 9-9b in *Research Methods: The Concise Knowledge Base*

1. How would you interpret the graph (i.e., what happened in the two groups from pre- to posttest)?

2. What are the alternative explanations for the outcome observed? Which threats to validity are most likely to influence the results?

Exercise 9-3b Designing Your Own Quasi-Experiment

After some study and a bit of practice, you may be ready to try designing your own experiment in the area of your interest. Use the following questions as a guide in considering the alternatives and the relative strengths and weaknesses they may bring to your study.

Step 1. What is the simplest quasi-experimental design you could use in your study? Write it in symbolic form. What hypothesis can you test with this design? What are the major alternative explanations for your possible outcomes? Try to draw a plot of the alternative outcomes.

Step 2. What threats to internal validity do you see in the simplest design? Use the following checklist to identify them and then write some notes about how likely you think these threats are to be in your particular study. Which threats appear to be most important for your study? Consider the following additions to your design.

Internal Validity Threat Checklist:

___ History   ___ Selection-Testing

___ Maturation   ___ Selection-Instrumentation

___ Testing   ___ Selection-Mortality

___ Instrumentation   ___ Selection-Regression

___ Mortality   ___ Diffusion or imitation

___ Regression to the mean   ___ Compensatory equalization

___ Selection   ___ Compensatory rivalry

___ Selection-History   ___ Resentful demoralization

___ Selection-Maturation

1. **Time.** What if you expand the number of observations over time? What impact will increasing observations over time have on control of internal validity? What about practical considerations, including access to your sample, cost, or unexpected complications such as new threats (e.g., mortality)?

2. **Conditions.** What if you increase the number of possible levels of one of your independent variables? You could add another kind of comparison group; increase or decrease the amount of exposure to a condition; or change setting, instruction, or other features of your independent variables.

3. **Observations.** What if you add additional observations or dependent measures? What might you be able to learn from a second or third kind of observation? For example, will a pretest help by providing you with a covariate or possibly hurt by producing a testing threat? Are there specific threats to validity you can try to control in this way? What practical limits are there for this kind of change in your design?

9-4 PRODUCTS

The products from this chapter should include the following:

1. At least one possible quasi-experimental design that you could use in your own study

2. A list of potential threats to the internal validity of your study

3. A set of alternative design possibilities to help control threats to internal validity

9-5 JOURNAL

In this chapter, you had practice considering quasi-experimental design strategies. You should now review and rate yourself on the competencies listed in the following self-evaluation.

Exercise 9-5a Research Methods Quasi-Experimental Design Self-Efficacy Evaluation

Use the following scale to rate your skills in each of the areas listed.

1 = Little or no ability to perform this task
2 = Some ability to perform this task
3 = Moderately good ability to perform this task
4 = Very good ability to perform this task
5 = Excellent ability to perform this task

1. _____ Understand and communicate the key terms in quasi-experimental research design and internal validity.

2. _____ Understand and communicate the key concepts in quasi-experimental research design and its relationship to internal validity.

3. _____ Identify the components of a quasi-experimental research design.

4. _____ Recognize a quasi-experimental research design written in design notation.

5. _____ Write a quasi-experimental research design in standard design notation.

6. _____ Identify a possible quasi-experimental design for a research question.

7. _____ Identify the threats to the internal validity of a quasi-experimental design proposal.

Exercise 9-5b Research Methods Quasi-Experimental Design Self-Evaluation

In the space provided, jot down your personal reactions to Chapter 9, "Quasi-Experimental Design," of *Resarch Methods: The Concise Knowledge Base*. What did you like best? What did you still need to study? How might you now improve your skills in quasi-experimental design?

10

Designing Designs

Chapter Outline

10-1 THE LANGUAGE OF DESIGNING DESIGNS

Exercise 10-1a The Key Terms *Preview*

Instructions. This exercise should be done before you read the chapter. Read every term in the Key Terms list. Now go back through the list again and identify up to 10 terms that you are unsure of so that you can pay special attention to them as you read. If you find that the entire list of key terms is unfamiliar, you should plan to read the chapter more than once and complete this exercise more than once as well. Write your preview terms in the following spaces:

Term 1:_____

Term 2:_____

Term 3:_____

Term 4:_____

Term 5:_____

Term 6:_____

Term 7:_____

Term 8:_____

Term 9:_____

Term 10:_____

Exercise 10-1b The Key Terms *Review*

Instructions. This exercise should be done after you read the chapter. The idea here is to see how much you've picked up to help you with the key terms you identified in your preview exercise. In the following spaces, write definitions of the terms in your own words. Try your best to do them by memory, but if you need to look them up again, go ahead and do so.

Term 1:_____ Definition:_____

_____

Term 2:_____ Definition: _____

_____

Term 3:_____ Definition: _____

_____

Term 4:_____ Definition: _____

_____

Term 5:_____ Definition: _____

_____

Term 6:_____ Definition: _____

_____

Term 7:_____ Definition: _____

_____

Term 8:_____ Definition: _____

_____

Term 9:_____ Definition: _____

_____

Term 10: _____ Definition: _____

_____

10-2 CONCEPTS

Exercise 10-2a Understanding and Communicating Key Ideas

Instructions. This exercise can be used to help you understand passages in *Research Methods: The Concise Knowledge Base*. You will need a partner for this exercise. Ideally, your partner would be a classmate in your research methods course or an advanced student. If a classmate or other fellow student is not available, you may try the exercise with another willing person. Feel free to draw pictures or make up examples to help you explain the idea.

1. **Identify** a passage in Chapter 10, "Designing Designs," of *Research Methods: The Concise Knowledge Base* that you would like to understand better. Keep in mind that if you are unsure of several parts of the chapter, do the earlier ones first because understanding the latter ones might depend on how well you understand the earlier ones.

2. **Read** the passage aloud to your partner. You may read it more than once if your partner requests you to do so.

3. **Discuss** the passage. Ask your partner to tell you what she or he heard in her or his own words. Give your partner feedback about what you think is the accuracy of her or his comment. If you discover discrepancies between your understanding and your partner's, read the passage aloud again.

4. **Write** the passage in the space provided. You and your partner should write a summary of the passage in your own words. After you have finished writing, read your passage to your partner and then allow your partner to take a turn.

5. **Conclusion.** You and your partner should now ask the question, "OK, now do we get it?" The evidence of improvement is your mutual understanding, your ability to discuss the passage orally, and your ability to write a brief summary. If you find that the passage is still unclear, well, that's what professors, email, and questions are for!

10-3 SKILLS

Exercise 10-3a Identifying Design Components and the Rationale for Their Use

Instructions. In this exercise, you will see a number of research designs from *Research Methods: The Concise Knowledge Base*. For each design, you will be asked to identify the components of the design and some reasons that they might be used in studies.

Design 1

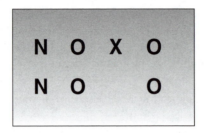

1. What would you call this design?

2. How many time points does the design have?

3. How many programs, treatments, or independent variables does the design have?

4. How many measures of each group does the design have?

5. How many groups of participants does the design have?

6. What is the research question this design addresses?

Design 2

(Notice that this design is an expansion of the prior one.)

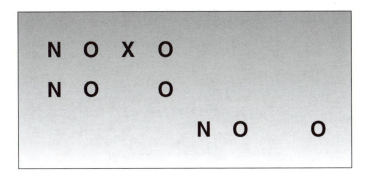

1. What would you call this design?

2. How many time points does the design have?

3. How many programs, treatments, or independent variables does the design have?

4. How many measures of each group does the design have?

5. How many groups of participants does the design have?

6. What is the research question this design addresses?

7. What additional advantages does this design provide over the prior one?

8. What additional costs or complications might be involved in implementing this design?

Exercise 10-3b Designing Your Own Design

At this point, you have the opportunity to "design your own design" and to consider the alternatives. Follow the steps outlined in this exercise to practice Professor Trochim's method, and you should end up with a reasonable possibility for your own study.

Step 1. Start with the simplest design. You start with a single cause and effect, as illustrated here.

What cause (the X or independent variable) are you interested in?

What effect (the O or dependent variable) are you interested in?

Step 2. Expand the design across time. In this step, you should consider the potential usefulness of a pretest (one or more) as well as a longer term follow-up measure (at least one).

    a. What would be the advantages of additional measure over time for the phenomenon you are studying, especially with regard to threats to the validity of your study?

    b. What would be the costs and limits of such expansion across time?

    c. In the space provided, sketch out a couple of alternative expansions over time and note the pros and cons associated with each alternative.

Step 3. Expand across programs or treatments. In this step, you are invited to consider alternative ways of presenting the treatment or program (the independent variable). Try to identify alternatives that might involve the following:

    a. Can you vary (increase or decrease) the amount of exposure (dosage, intensity, strength) of the treatment or program?

    b. Can you use a theory to suggest an alternative that would have a different outcome (maybe even the opposite) of the one you are predicting from your treatment?

 c. Can you identify and vary the parts of the program that you might consider to be the key or most "active ingredients"?

 d. In the space provided, sketch a couple of alternatives and note the pros and cons of expanding across programs or treatments.

Step 4. Expand across observations. In this step, you are invited to think about the potential advantages and costs of expanding your study by adding additional observations or measures. Carefully consider whether any of the following might add substantially to your study:

 a. Could you add a second measure of the same construct to add the perspective of another observer (e.g., a parent, sibling, or professional person)?

 b. Could you add an additional measure that would give you an alternative measurement strategy (e.g., something objective as well as subjective)?

 c. Could you add a retrospective pretest? That is, if you did not have a pretest, could you ask participants to respond to questions from the perspective of how they felt or were thinking before the study?

 d. In the space provided, sketch a couple of alternatives and note the pros and cons of expanding across programs or treatments.

Step 5. Expand across groups. One of the best ways to address the common problem of selection bias is to add additional groups to the study. Consider additional comparisons that could be made such as the following:

 a. Can you compare your groups to a standardized set of norms for your measure or measures?

b. Can you add a second comparison group that might have some key variables in common with your primary treatment group but differ in a specific way? Adding such a group would be particularly advantageous if the two groups do not have regular contact with each other (i.e., they are independent of one another).

c. Can you combine random assignment with a cutoff score to create sub-groups that might be helpful in isolating certain effects, ruling out alternative explanations, or limiting threats to validity?

d. In the space provided, sketch a couple of alternatives and note the pros and cons of expanding across programs or treatments.

Step 6. Critique and integrate your design. At this point, you may have several additions to your basic design. In fact, if you were to combine them all into one design, it may be quite complex and perhaps not a realistic alternative. However, the basic idea of overexpanding the design elements is parallel to the hourglass concept presented in Chapter 1, "Foundations." You start broadly, consider all the possibilities, and then narrow your focus to a specific question based on a critical and well-informed perspective. At this point, you should review all the possible alternatives you've considered and then begin trying to put them together into an integrated design. As you review the alternatives, you will need to consider such issues as ethics, cost, access, and whether you may be able to justify a simpler design through control of validity concerns via argument, measurement, analysis, or preventive action of some kind. In the space provided, try to identify one or two "finalists" for your study. Then weigh the alternatives based on scientific and practical criteria. After you have completed this step, you will have followed the process of study design to a key choice point. In real life, researchers aren't always so systematic, which is one reason that you find so many studies that seem to do the same thing over and over again. Perhaps you'll come up with a new design that might provide the possibility of new insight!

10-4 PRODUCTS

The products from this chapter should include the following:

1. At least one possible design that you could use in your own study
2. A list of potential threats to the validity of your study
3. A critical analysis of the ethical and practical constraints on your alternative designs
4. A set of alternative design possibilities to help control threats to validity

10-5 JOURNAL

In this chapter, you had practice considering design strategies. You should now review and rate yourself on the competencies listed in the following self-evaluation.

Exercise 10-5a Research Methods Designing Designs Self-Efficacy Evaluation

Use the following scale to rate your skills in each of the areas listed.

1 = Little or no ability to perform this task
2 = Some ability to perform this task
3 = Moderately good ability to perform this task
4 = Very good ability to perform this task
5 = Excellent ability to perform this task

1. _____ Understand and communicate the key terms in designing designs.

2. _____ Understand and communicate the key concepts in designing designs.

3. _____ Identify the components of a research design.

4. _____ Recognize a research design written in design notation.

5. _____ Write a research design in standard design notation.

6. _____ Identify at least one possible design for a research question.

7. _____ Identify the threats to the validity of alternative designs.

Exercise 10-5b Research Methods Designing Designs
Self-Evaluation

In the space provided, jot down your personal reactions to Chapter 10, "Designing Designs," of *Research Methods: The Concise Knowledge Base*. What did you like best? What did you still need to study? How might you now improve your skills in designing designs?

ANALYSIS

11

Analysis

Chapter Outline

11-1 THE LANGUAGE OF ANALYSIS

Exercise 11-1a The Key Terms *Preview*

Instructions. This exercise should be done before you read the chapter. Read every term in the Key Terms list. Now go back through the list again and identify up to 10 terms that you are unsure of so that you can pay special attention to them as you read. If you find that the entire list of key terms is unfamiliar, you should plan to read the chapter more than once and complete this exercise more than once as well. Write your preview terms in the following spaces:

Term 1:_____

Term 2:_____

Term 3:_____

Term 4:_____

Term 5:_____

Term 6:_____

Term 7:_____

Term 8:_____

Term 9:_____

Term 10:_____

Exercise 11-1b The Key Terms *Review*

Instructions. This exercise should be done after you read the chapter. The idea here is to see how much you've picked up to help you with the key terms you identified in your preview exercise. In the following spaces, write definitions of the terms in your own words. Try your best to do them by memory, but if you need to look them up again, go ahead and do so.

Term 1:_____ Definition: _____

_____

Term 2: _____ Definition: _____

_____

Term 3: _____ Definition: _____

_____

Term 4: _____ Definition: _____

_____

Term 5: _____ Definition: _____

_____

Term 6: _____ Definition: _____

_____

Term 7: _____ Definition: _____

_____

Term 8: _____ Definition: _____

_____

Term 9: _____ Definition: _____

_____

Term 10: _____ Definition: _____

_____

11-2 CONCEPTS

Exercise 11-2a Understanding and Communicating Key Ideas

Instructions. This exercise can be used to help you understand passages in *Research Methods: The Concise Knowledge Base*. You will need a partner for this exercise. Ideally, your partner would be a classmate in your research methods course or an advanced student. If a classmate or other fellow student is not available, you may try the exercise with another willing person. Feel free to draw pictures or make up examples to help you explain the idea.

1. **Identify** a passage in Chapter 11, "Analysis," of *Research Methods: The Concise Knowledge Base* that you would like to understand better. Keep in mind that if you are unsure of several parts of the chapter, do the earlier ones first because understanding the latter ones might depend on how well you understand the earlier ones.

2. **Read** the passage aloud to your partner. You may read it more than once if your partner requests you to do so.

3. **Discuss** the passage. Ask your partner to tell you what she or he heard in her or his own words. Give your partner feedback about what you think is the accuracy of her or his comment. If you discover discrepancies in your understanding and your partner's, read the passage aloud again.

4. **Write** the passage in the space provided. You and your partner should write a summary of the passage in your own words. After you have finished writing, read your passage to your partner and then allow your partner to take a turn.

5. **Conclusion.** You and your partner should now ask the question, "OK, now do we get it?" The evidence of improvement is your mutual understanding, your ability to discuss the passage orally, and your ability to write a brief summary. If you find that the passage is still unclear, well, that's what professors, email, and questions are for!

Exercise 11-2b Understanding Statistical Significance and Power

The following fill-in-the-blank items will help you review your understanding of the concepts of statistical significance and power discussed in the chapter.

1. Determining the number of participants for a study can be done in a systematic and formal way by conducting a _____ analysis.

2. The four things you need to know to conduct a power analysis in planning a study are

   a. _____

   b. _____

   c. _____

   d. _____

3. A Type I error occurs when we say there _____ an effect or relationship when in fact there is none.

4. The Type I error rate is usually set by the researcher in advance and is traditionally set to _____.

5. The Type I error rate is also known as the _____ error rate.

6. A Type II error occurs when we say there _____ an effect or relationship when in fact there is one.

7. Power is the odds of saying there _____ an effect when in fact there is one. Power levels are often set to be _____.

8. The confidence level is the odds of saying there _____ an effect or relationship when in fact there is none.

9. The lower the alpha, the _____ the power. The higher the alpha, the _____ the power.

10. The _____ the alpha, the more rigorous the test.

11. An alpha of .01 means the researcher is being more _____ than she would be if she used an alpha of .05.

12. An alpha of .05 means that the researcher is willing to accept being wrong _____ times out of 100 in rejecting a null hypothesis that is actually true (saying there _____ an effect when in fact there is not).

13. An alpha of .01 compared to .05 gives you _____ statistical power along with _____ odds of making a Type I error.

14. An alpha of .05 means there is a _____% chance of saying there is no difference (or no relationship) when in fact there is none.

15. Increasing alpha (e.g., from .01 to .05) _____ the chances of making a Type I error (saying there is a difference when there is not), _____ the chances of making a Type II error, and _____ the rigor of the test.

11-3 SKILLS

Exercise 11-3a Determining the Order of Steps to Prepare Data for Analysis

Instructions. In this exercise, you'll see the recommended steps for preparing a dataset for analysis, but the order is incorrect. Your task is to number them in the proper order.

_____ Conduct data transformations (e.g., add substitute values for missing data or do any item reversals that are needed).

_____ Create your codebook.

_____ Check the data for accuracy.

_____ Calculate total or other scale scores from the items.

_____ Log the data records as they are received (e.g., your surveys).

Exercise 11-3b Interpreting a Table of Descriptive Statistics

Instructions. In this exercise, you will see a table of descriptive statistics for a small set of test scores from *Research Methods: The Concise Knowledge Base*. Examine Table 11-1 and then use it to answer the questions that follow.

TABLE 11-1

Table of Descriptive Statistics

N	8
Mean	20.8750
Median	20.0000
Mode	15.00
Std. Deviation	7.0799
Variance	50.1250
Range	21.00

1. What was the average test score?

2. What was the most frequent test score?

3. What score divides the distribution in half (half above, half below)?

4. The _____, _____, and _____ tell you about the central tendency of the data.

5. Which numbers tell you about how much the test scores vary from one another?

6. What is the difference between the lowest and highest score in the dataset?

7. The _____ and _____ are determined by examining the deviation of each score from the mean of all the scores.

8. The deviation of each score from the mean is _____ (multiplied by itself), so that there are no negative numbers. These numbers can then be added and produce a value called the _____.

9. If this distribution was normal, you could estimate that _____ percent of the scores would fall in the interval from 6.7152 and 35.0348.

10. If this distribution was normal, you could estimate that 99 percent of the scores would fall in the interval from _____ to _____.

Exercise 11-3c Interpreting a Correlation Matrix

Instructions. In this exercise, you will see a correlation matrix. Examine the matrix and answer the questions that follow.

	V1	V2	V3	V4
V1	1.0			
V2	.27	1.0		
V3	–.13	.65	1.0	
V4	.20	–.15	–.72	1.0

1. Which two variables have the strongest (largest) relationship?

2. Which two variables have the weakest (smallest) relationship?

3. Which two variables have the strongest positive relationship?

4. Which two variables have the strongest negative relationship?

5. Which two variables have the weakest positive relationship?

6. Which two variables have the weakest negative relationship?

7. Which variables go down when V4 goes up?

8. Which variable is most likely to increase as V3 increases?

9. Draw a scatterplot that might roughly represent the correlation between V2 and V3.

10.   Draw a scatterplot that might roughly represent the correlation between V2 and V4.

11-4 PRODUCTS

The products from this chapter should include the following:

1. The necessary components of a power analysis to determine how many participants you will need for your study

2. A plan for managing your data so that it is well organized, "clean," and ready for analysis

3. A plan for your initial set of data analyses, including checking data accuracy and examining the descriptive statistics

11-5 JOURNAL

In this chapter, you had practice considering strategies for analyzing your data. You should now review and rate yourself on the competencies listed in the following self-evaluation.

Exercise 11-5a Research Methods Analysis Self-Efficacy Evaluation

Use the following scale to rate your skills in each of the areas listed.

1 = Little or no ability to perform this task
2 = Some ability to perform this task
3 = Moderately good ability to perform this task
4 = Very good ability to perform this task
5 = Excellent ability to perform this task

1. _____ Identify the elements of a power analysis.

2. _____ Organize and manage data.

3. _____ Write a codebook.

4. _____ Check data for accuracy.

5. _____ Determine which descriptive statistics should be examined.

6. _____ Calculate central tendency and variability statistics.

7. _____ Calculate a correlation coefficient.

8. _____ Interpret a table of descriptive statistics.

9. _____ Interpret a correlation matrix.

Exercise 11-5b Research Methods Analysis
Self-Evaluation

In the space provided, jot down your personal reactions to Chapter 11, "Analysis," of *Research Methods: The Concise Knowledge Base*. What did you like best? What did you still need to study? How might you now improve your skills in analysis?

12

Analysis for Research Design

Chapter Outline

12-1 THE LANGUAGE OF ANALYSIS FOR RESEARCH DESIGN

Exercise 12-1a The Key Terms *Preview*

Instructions. This exercise should be done before you read the chapter. Read every term in the Key Terms list. Now go back through the list again and identify up to 10 terms that you are unsure of so that you can pay special attention to them as you read. If you find that the entire list of key terms is unfamiliar, you should plan to read the chapter more than once and complete this exercise more than once as well. Write your preview terms in the following spaces:

Term 1:_____

Term 2:_____

Term 3:_____

Term 4:_____

Term 5:_____

Term 6:_____

Term 7:_____

Term 8:_____

Term 9:_____

Term 10:_____

Exercise 12-1b The Key Terms *Review*

Instructions. This exercise should be done after you read the chapter. The idea here is to see how much you've picked up to help you with the key terms you identified in your preview exercise. In the following spaces, write definitions of the terms in your own words. Try your best to do them by memory, but if you need to look them up again, go ahead and do so.

Term 1:_____ Definition: _____

_____

Term 2:_____ Definition: _____

_____

Term 3:_____ Definition: _____

_____

Term 4:_____ Definition: _____

_____

Term 5:_____ Definition: _____

_____

Term 6:_____ Definition: _____

_____

Term 7:_____ Definition: _____

_____

Term 8:_____ Definition: _____

_____

Term 9:_____ Definition:_____

_____

Term 10:_____ Definition: _____

_____

12-2 CONCEPTS

Exercise 12-2a Understanding and Communicating Key Ideas

Instructions. This exercise can be used to help you understand passages in *Research Methods: The Concise Knowledge Base*. You will need a partner for this exercise. Ideally, your partner would be a classmate in your research methods course or an advanced student. If a classmate or other fellow student is not available, you may try the exercise with another willing person. Feel free to draw pictures or make up examples to help you explain the idea.

1. **Identify** a passage in Chapter 12, "Analysis for Research Design," of *Research Methods: The Concise Knowledge Base* that you would like to understand better. Keep in mind that if you are unsure of several parts of the chapter, do the earlier ones first because understanding the latter ones might depend on how well you understand the earlier ones.

2. **Read** the passage aloud to your partner. You may read it more than once if your partner requests you to do so.

3. **Discuss** the passage. Ask your partner to tell you what she or he heard in her or his own words. Give your partner feedback about what you think is the accuracy of her or his comment. If you discover discrepancies between your understanding and your partner's, read the passage aloud again.

4. **Write** the passage in the space provided. You and your partner should write a summary of the passage in your own words. After you have finished writing, read your passage to your partner and then allow your partner to take a turn.

5. **Conclusion.** You and your partner should now ask the question, "OK, now do we get it?" The evidence of improvement is your mutual understanding, your ability to discuss the passage orally, and your ability to write a brief summary. If you find that the passage is still unclear, well, that's what professors, email, and questions are for!

Exercise 12-2b Checking Your Understanding
of Key Concepts

Instructions. The following sentence-completion items should help you check your comprehension of the concepts presented in this chapter.

1. The general _____ model is the most widely used statistical model.

2. The line that best fits a bivariate distribution (as you would see in a scatterplot of an x and a y) is called the _____ line.

3. If you had a two-group (e.g., a treatment group and a control group) experimental design and wanted to know whether the means of the groups were significantly different, you could use a ___ test.

4. When you use inferential statistics (such as the *t*-test, anova, or regression analysis) to examine the signal-to-noise ratio in a study, the signal is the _____ between the groups, and the noise is the _____ of the groups.

5. If you have a randomized experimental design and included a pretest, you will probably analyze the data using an analysis of _____.

6. When a treatment group and control group are coded with values such as "1" and "0," we say the variable has been _____ coded.

7. Analysis of data from a quasi-experiment is more complicated than analysis of a true experiment because of the likelihood of _____ results if the data is not adjusted for the reliability of the measures.

The following questions are related to the equation for the general linear model:

$$y_i = \beta_0 + \beta_1 Z_1 + e_i$$

1. In the equation, the outcome score (the dependent variable) is represented by _____.

2. In the equation, the e_i term represents the variance that cannot be estimated from the data and is called the _____.

3. The part of the equation that tells you the amount of change in the dependent variable relative to the change in the independent variable is _____, which is the coefficient for the _____ of the regression line.

12-3 SKILLS

Exercise 12-3a Interpreting the Results of an Inferential Statistical Analysis

In this exercise, we'll revisit the results of the health risk behavior survey presented previously to get some practice in examining the kinds of results you would get from the analyses presented in the chapter. For each example, you will see the output of a statistical program and then be asked a series of questions related to interpretation of the results.

Do boys and girls differ in the amount of TV they watch?

In this analysis, we'll compare the average number of hours boys and girls watch TV per day. In Table 12-1, we'll look at the descriptive statistics, and then in Table 12-2, we'll look at the *t*-test results.

	What is your sex?	N	Mean	Std. Deviation	Std. Error Mean
How many hours do you watch TV?	Female	6786	4.14	1.797	.022
	Male	6417	4.30	1.758	.022

TABLE 12-1

Number of Hours Spent Watching Television

1. How many females were in the study?

2. How many males were in the study?

3. What was the average number of hours females watched television?

4. What was the average number of hours males watched television?

TABLE 12-2   *t*-test Results of Inferential Statistical Analysis

				t-test for Equality of Means			
	t	*df*	Sig. (2-tailed)	Mean Difference	Std. Error Difference	95% Confidence Interval of the Difference	
						Lower	Upper
How many hours do you watch TV?	5.185	13201	.000	−.16	.031	−.221	−.100

1. What was the value of the *t*-statistic for this analysis?

2. What was the estimated probability associated with this result (the significance level)?

3. What was the estimated difference between the females and males?

4. Do you think the difference between the females and males is meaningful (i.e., does this amount of TV watching matter)?

5. Was the difference statistically significant?

6. Is your opinion of the meaningfulness of the difference consistent with the statistical results? If not, what might account for the difference in the two interpretations of the data?

7. What would be the 95% confidence interval for this difference?

    95% CI = mean difference +/– 2(standard error of the difference)

Exercise 12-3b Planning the Analysis of Your Data

If you have been developing a proposal for research in this course, you may need to include a plan for the analysis of your data. This might be the section of your paper called "Statistical Considerations." In this exercise, your task is to identify an analysis that could test the hypothesis you have developed. Of course, some studies are purely descriptive or exploratory and will not attempt to conduct significance tests to answer a research question. However, Chapter 12, "Analysis for Research Design," provides a basic introduction to the kinds of analyses you could use if you were planning a hypothesis test based on inferential statistical procedures. In the space provided, write one of the hypotheses you are interested in testing in your study and then note whether a t-test, analysis of variance or covariance, or regression analysis might be applicable. Writing out the general formula for the statistical model you are considering will help your understanding.

12-4 PRODUCTS

The products from this chapter should include the following:

1. An understanding of the difference between descriptive and inferential statistics

2. An introductory knowledge of the use of the general linear model in inferential statistics

3. A basic understanding of the comparability of different ways of analyzing data based on the general linear model (e.g., the correspondence of an analysis of variance to a regression analysis)

4. A basic introduction to the complexity of analyzing quasi-experimental designs compared with randomized experiments

5. A tentative plan for testing your own study hypothesis with inferential statistical procedures

12-5 JOURNAL

In this chapter, you had practice considering analysis strategies for research design. You should now review and rate yourself on the competencies listed in the following self-evaluation.

Exercise 12-5a Research Methods Analysis for Research Design Self-Efficacy Evaluation

Use the following scale to rate your skills in each of the areas listed.

1 = Little or no ability to perform this task
2 = Some ability to perform this task
3 = Moderately good ability to perform this task
4 = Very good ability to perform this task
5 = Excellent ability to perform this task

1. _____ Identify research questions that could be answered with inferential statistics.

2. _____ Identify the components of the general linear model.

3. _____ Identify at least one inferential statistical procedure that could be used in your study.

4. _____ Explain what the 95% confidence interval is.

5. _____ Interpret the results of an inferential statistical analysis.

6. _____ Critically evaluate the difference between statistical and practical significance (meaningfulness).

Exercise 12-5b Research Methods Analysis for Research Design Self-Evaluation

In the space provided, jot down your personal reactions to Chapter 12, "Analysis for Research Design," of *Research Methods: The Concise Knowledge Base*. What did you like best? What did you still need to study? How might you now improve your skills in analysis for research design?

13

Write-Up

At this point, you have been introduced to all the basic terminology of science that you will learn in this book. But as noted in *Research Methods: The Concise Knowledge Base*, your work is far from complete! Writing (and presenting) research findings could be the subject of an entire book, and in fact, it has been the topic of many. This final workbook chapter will maintain the general structure of language, concepts, skill, products, and self-evaluation, but it will look just a bit different, beginning with the section on language.

13-1 THE LANGUAGE OF WRITING RESEARCH FINDINGS

Exercise 13-1a The Key Terms

In this exercise, you will practice identifying proper use of some key terms in scientific writing. These terms are frequently used and frequently *misused*. We hope that by recognizing proper use early in your writing career, you will form good habits and save yourself from your professor's red pencil (or the electronic equivalent).

Instructions. For each sentence, choose the form of the word that correctly completes the sentence.

1. The results of the study indicated that there was no significant _____ of age on test scores.

   a. effect
   b. affect
   c. difference
   d. variance

2. The data _____ that further study is warranted.

   a. suggest
   b. suggests
   c. reveal
   d. prove

3. The client had _____ symptoms after three months of counseling.

   a. fewer
   b. less
   c. smaller
   d. better

4. The subjects will be provided with compensation for their participation in the study, _____ of whether they complete all the study sessions.

   a. regardless
   b. irregardless
   c. contingent
   d. dependent

5. The causal variable is the one that _____ the dependent variable.

   a. affects
   b. effects
   c. supports
   d. correlates

6. The _____ of participants in the study was too small to have adequate statistical power.

   a. amount
   b. number
   c. quality
   d. quantity

7. In their early work, Smith and Jones (1976) _____ that completion of research methods exercises was significantly related to course grade.

    a. reported
    b. report
    c. mention
    d. confirm

8. The analysis showed that persistence was correlated _____ success.

    a. to
    b. with
    c. from
    d. among

9. The _____ for eligibility included ability to read and speak English and being at least 18 years of age.

    a. criteria
    b. criterion
    c. experience
    d. participants

10. The purpose of this study was to investigate the relationship _____ family environment and career maturity.

    a. among
    b. between
    c. within
    d. perspective

13-2 PRESENTING CONCEPTS

Exercise 13-2a Understanding and Communicating Key Ideas

Instructions. This exercise is similar to the ones that you have practiced in previous chapters, except that the goal here is to help you master the literature you have been studying instead of *Research Methods: The Concise Knowledge Base* concepts by communicating with another person. This time you can do the exercise with an individual, a small group, or with your entire class. After you have explained key concepts to others, you should be in a good position to write about them in your literature review.

1. **Identify** a passage in one of the articles you have collected in your literature review. It should be one that you will cite in your review because it is central to understanding the area of study. This means it should include the major concepts, constructs, or variables that you want to study.

2. **Verbally present** the passage aloud to your partner. In this step, you will try to concisely explain the idea to your partner or group.

3. **Ask for feedback and discuss** the passage. Ask your partner to tell you what she or he heard in her or his own words. If your partner has questions, try to answer them from what you believe is the point of view of the author.

4. **Summarize the discussion.** At this point, you should try to summarize the discussion of the idea, including integration of the follow-up questions. You might now have a list of issues or unresolved questions that you would like to follow up on to enhance your understanding. You can use the space provided to record the questions or issues for follow-up.

5. **Conclusion.** You and your partner should now ask the question, "OK, now do we get it?" The evidence of improvement is your mutual understanding, your ability to discuss the passage orally, and the quality of the follow-up discussion. If you find that the passage is still unclear, you may need to study the article or articles further or find and read related work.

13-3 SKILLS

Exercise 13-3a Writing Up the Results of an Inferential Statistical Analysis

Once again, we'll revisit the health risk behavior survey presented in Chapter 2, "Sampling," to get some practice in writing up the results of a hypothesis test. We'll review the results shown previously, but here your job will be to put your interpretation in writing.

The research question was: "Do boys and girls differ in the amount of TV they watch?"

In this analysis, we compared the average number of hours boys and girls watched TV per day. We looked at the descriptive statistics shown in Table 13-1 and then the *t*-test results shown in Table 13-2.

TABLE 13-1

Number of Hours Spent Watching Television

	What is your sex?	N	Mean	Std. Deviation	Std. Error Mean
How many hours do you watch TV?	Female	6786	4.14	1.797	.022
	Male	6417	4.30	1.758	.022

TABLE 13-2   *t*-test Results of Inferential Statistical Analysis

						95% Confidence Interval of the Difference	
	t	*df*	Sig. (2-tailed)	Mean Difference	Std. Error Difference	Lower	Upper
How many hours do you watch TV?	5.185	13201	.000	−.16	.031	−.221	−.100

t-test for Equality of Means

In the space provided, write a paragraph summarizing the results of this analysis. Your write-up should include either a table or a graph formatted in APA style.

13-4 PRODUCTS

In this final chapter, we anticipate that many students will be focused on trying to complete THE major product of the research methods course: a literature review and/or proposal for research. We have therefore added an additional item to this chapter: a checklist that you can use to assess the completeness of your own paper. The checklist is based on the items described in *Research Methods: The Concise Knowledge Base*.

Instructions. When you have a draft of your paper, use the checklist to review each section and determine whether your paper addresses each issue.

I. Introduction

    1. Statement of the problem

        ____ The statement of the problem is clear and unambiguous.

        ____ The importance and significance of the problem are described.

    2. Statement of causal relationship

        ____ The cause-effect relationship has been identified and discussed in relation to the current study.

    3. Statement of constructs

        ____ Each key construct has been explained in a clear, jargon-free manner.

    4. Literature citations and review

        ____ The literature search procedures have been clearly described.

        ____ Literature has been summarized in a critical but fair manner.

        ____ All literature cited is relevant to the study.

        ____ All citations are properly formatted.

    5. Statement of hypothesis

        ____ The hypothesis (or hypotheses) of the study is (are) clearly stated.

        ____ The hypothesis is justified by the literature review.

II. Methods

    1. Sample section

        ____ The sampling procedure (the participants, cases, or records) is clearly described (so that another researcher could replicate it exactly).

        ____ The population is clearly defined.

        ____ The sampling frame is clearly described.

    2. Sample description

        ____ Relevant characteristics of the sample are detailed.

        ____ Issues related to external validity (e.g., known potential biases such as mortality) are described clearly as well as methods of attempting to control or limit such threats.

        ____ The response rate is provided.

        ____ Missing data is discussed in detail.

    3. Measurement section

    If previously published measures are to be used:

        ____ Each measurement construct has been described briefly.

        ____ The measure to be used for each construct has been adequately identified (the citation for the measure is complete, and the measure is attached to the paper as an appendix).

        ____ Multiple measures for each construct have been used (if possible).

If previously published or collected data is to be used:

___ The measurement procedures, including the scaling methods, are described.

If new measures are to be used:

___ Items or questions are appropriate for the population.

___ Items or questions are organized in a logical manner.

___ Questions or items are carefully and clearly written.

If qualitative measures are to be used:

___ Details of qualitative data collection and coding are provided.

Reliability and validity

___ Reliability evidence is provided for each measure, including what estimation procedures were used.

___ Construct validity is addressed.

___ Evidence of convergent and discriminant validity is provided.

4. Design and Procedures section

___ The design is clearly described in text.

___ The design is clearly described in notation form.

___ The design is appropriate for the research problem.

___ Threats to internal validity have been addressed in the design.

___ Threats to internal validity that are not addressed by the design are considered in terms of impact on interpretation of results.

___ Statistical power is considered for the proposed analysis.

___ All study procedures are completely described so that another researcher could replicate them.

___ Ethical considerations are discussed as well as procedures to address them.

III. Results (actual or anticipated)

___ Results are presented in relation to the hypotheses tested or problems addressed.

___ Assumptions of all data analysis procedures are discussed (e.g., normality of distributions).

___ Sufficient descriptive statistics are presented to enable the reader to become familiar with central tendency and variability of the measures.

___ Tables and figures are formatted concisely and in accord with style manual guidelines.

___ Only necessary tables and graphs are included (additional supporting data may be added to an appendix).

___ All tables and figures are discussed in the text of the results.

___ Confidence intervals and effect sizes are provided.

IV. Discussion

___ A summary statement integrating the literature review and results of the study is provided.

___ Implications for theory, practice, and future research are discussed.

___ Limitations of the study are acknowledged.

V. References

___ All references are provided (and only those works cited in the paper) consistent with the style manual guidelines.

Writing Style Checklist

___ Language used does not show bias toward any group discussed.

___ Writing is interesting but not emotional or presented from a first person perspective (e.g., "I feel that this is the most important problem in the world and I'm very upset about it.").

___ Tense is parallel and consistent (e.g., past tense when discussing research that has been completed).

___ Spelling has been checked (via a program and a human reader).

___ Grammar has been checked (via a program and a human reader).

___ All stylistic conventions have otherwise been followed (see the style manual in your field).

The products from this chapter should include the following:

1. Knowledge of some frequently misused terms in scientific writing

2. Understanding of key concepts in the area of literature that you have reviewed

3. Understanding of the sections of a research paper

4. An outline of your own literature review, research proposal, or empirical report

5. A checklist assessment of your paper in relation to the qualities of a well-written paper

13-5 JOURNAL

In this chapter, you had practice with various aspects of writing up a research study. You should now review and rate yourself on the competencies listed in the following self-evaluation.

Exercise 13-5a Writing Self-Efficacy Evaluation

Use the following scale to rate your skills in each of the areas listed.

1 = Little or no ability to perform this task
2 = Some ability to perform this task
3 = Moderately good ability to perform this task
4 = Very good ability to perform this task
5 = Excellent ability to perform this task

1. ____ Report on the results of a literature review.

2. ____ Write a proposal for research.

3. ____ Report on the results of a study that I will conduct.

4. ____ Use APA style properly.

Exercise 13-5b Research Methods Writing
Self-Evaluation

In the space provided, jot down your personal reactions to Chapter 13, "Write-Up," of *Research Methods: The Concise Knowledge Base*. What did you like best? What did you still need to study? How might you now improve your skills in writing?